GREAT TEACHERS
MAKE A DIFFERENCE

GAINES S. DOBBINS

Great Teachers Make a Difference

BROADMAN PRESS
Nashville, Tennessee

DEWEY DECIMAL CLASSIFICATION: 920

Library of Congress catalog card number: 65–21199

Printed in the United States of America

13.5MY65KSP

To
MY WIFE
who with me knew and loved
the men these sketches seek to portray

Preface

Since teaching is an art, the teacher should be an artist. The artist is one who effectually communicates himself, his concepts, and his insights to others. The teacher's medium is personality expressing itself through language. The teacher, like any other artist, needs models. The study of these models is not just in order to imitate them, but to learn from them the skills to be employed and to receive from them the stimulation and guidance needed for success. Just as the painter or the musician studies the masters, so should the teacher study master teachers.

These sketches grew out of a series of lectures given at chapel services of Golden Gate Baptist Theological Seminary, Mill Valley, California. The generous response of faculty and students led to the elaboration of the chapel talks into this brief volume.

I was further urged to put these messages into print by the fact that not many now living enjoyed the privilege which was mine of being students of the men whom I have tried faithfully, though inadequately, to portray as great teachers.

As in the flesh they blessed the lives of countless students and others of the generation just passing, so may they bless the lives of the oncoming generation through these recollections of their teaching ministry.

I am indebted to several sources of more exact information than afforded by memory: John A. Broadus, *Memoir of James P. Boyce;* Isla May Mullins, *Edgar Young Mullins, an Intimate Biography;* John R. Sampey, *Memoirs;* Everett Gill, *A. T. Robertson, a Biography; Encyclopedia of Southern Baptists,* 2 vols.; *Religious Education,* Volume XLVII, Number 2, March–April, 1952.

Time and space do not permit the inclusion of other great teachers who equally deserve a place in these recollections. To pay tribute to them all would be a happy privilege yet impossible task.

GAINES S. DOBBINS

A Note from the Publisher

Gaines S. Dobbins himself has enjoyed a long and distinguished career as a teacher. As his many former students recognize, he has exhibited the qualities of greatness that he has observed in others. The publisher thus judged it appropriate to secure a chapter about his influence as a teacher. With his consent, this has been added to his original manuscript and appears below as Chapter 8. It has been provided by Wayne E. Oates, a former student of Dr. Dobbins, who is particularly qualified to write it by his own experience as a teacher and an author.

Contents

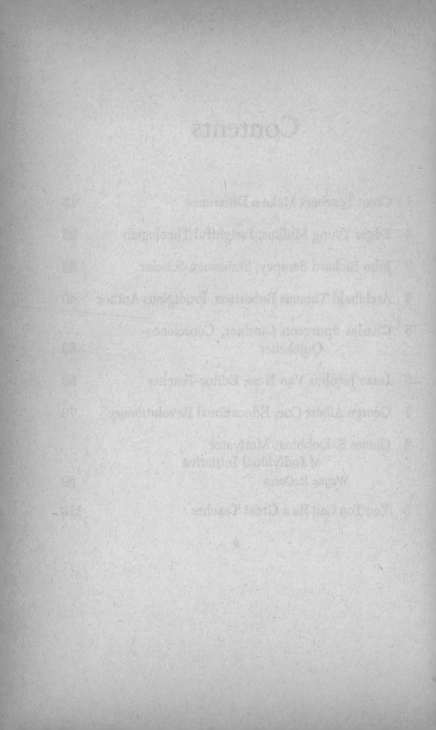

Contents

GREAT TEACHERS
MAKE A DIFFERENCE

1
Great Teachers Make a Difference

If any man's will is to do his will, he shall know whether the teaching is from God (John 7:17, RSV).

Horace Bushnell, author of the epoch-making *Christian Nurture,* held that more is done during the first three years to determine destiny than in the rest of life. Perhaps this is an overstatement, but it contains a significant element of truth. Whether he fully realizes it or not, every man's first and often greatest teacher is his mother. Abraham Lincoln said, "All that I am, or hope to be, I owe to my angel mother." Not every mother can be paid such tribute, but every mother is a teacher.

My earliest recollections are of my mother as teacher. We lived on a farm about four miles from the village school. My father and mother thought the distance was too great for a six-year-old to walk alone. So my mother, busy about the housework and with the "hands" to feed at noon, taught me letters and numbers and how to spell and read. When I entered school the next year, I was placed in the second grade.

My teacher was an exacting "old maid" who believed in strict discipline. She knew I was advanced but was not certain that I was advanced enough for second grade. She tested me with the multiplication tables. I did all right until I came to the nines. Realizing I couldn't do it, I sat down in confusion. Sternly she ordered me to my seat, telling me that if I could not go on through the twelve table she would have to put me back into first grade. When I protested she threatened to whip me.

Tearfully I told my mother the story. "Please," I begged, "don't make me go back until I can pass the test." This was on Friday. Mother drilled me patiently and incessantly on tables nine to twelve, until on Monday I stood before the teacher and rattled them off letter-perfect! Mother took for granted that I could do anything the other children could do and made me believe it. Her insight and confidence in me *made a lifelong difference*.

Later we moved to Hattiesburg, Mississippi—a growing town in the southern part of the state. Here I continued my schooling without incident. But when I entered high school, like many another boy, I grew tired of school and wanted to drop out. I was working after hours and on Saturdays in the printing office as apprentice or "printer's devil." We did job printing and published a weekly paper. The editor took a lively interest in me and the owner indicated that he could use me full time. I spoke to the high school superintendent—a kind, devout Methodist—about the possibility of leaving school. He took me into his office and earnestly expressed confidence in my future and urged me to continue in school. His encouragement and Mother's strong objection to my quitting turned the tide. I began to take a renewed interest in school and was particularly impressed by the daily chapel exercises led by Mr. Woodley, the superintendent. We lustily sang a hymn, listened to the Bible reading and prayer, and were led in brief religious devotions by the superintendent or one of the teachers. Through all the years ahead, the influence of this godly teacher would make a difference.

At the close of my third year in high school, my parents moved to a town about midway between Hattiesburg and Gulfport. My father was now a hotelkeeper and went to take over the hotel in this boomtown.

By now I was a fairly competent printer and secured work in the local printing office. The editor-proprietor took his responsibility lightly and soon I found myself doing most of the work in the office and getting out the paper. The town boom did not materialize and my parents moved back to Hattiesburg. I agreed to stay on and work in the printing office until school reopened in the fall.

It was my last week in the printing office. I had run off the weekly edition of the paper and was taking the form to the rack for washing before distributing the type for the next edition. In those days, all the type was set by hand. Somehow my foot slipped, I put my knee through the "chase" containing the type and it "pied" all over the floor! As I stood regarding it in dismay, the proprietor came in, made the air lurid with his language, and ordered me to reset it before I left. On such apparent accidents often hangs destiny.

That very week there arrived in town the new superintendent of the public school. He was a graduate of Mississippi College and had just completed requirements for the Master's degree at Cornell University. He had learned that there would be only one senior student, a girl. He had talked to my boss, who wanted me to stay on and work in the printing office. Professor L. L. Patterson came to me with the proposal that I take the job and that I enrol as a senior in his school. The idea appealed to me and I gained my parents' reluctant consent to stay.

Professor Patterson, who was later to become the dean of the School of Engineering at Mississippi State, was a superb teacher. More than anything else, I enjoyed his introductory course in Greek. Soon we were reading the *Anabasis,* which marked the beginning of a lifelong interest in the Greek language and literature. Acquaintance with this great teacher changed the course of my life.

Returning home at the close of the session, I went back to work in the printing office. By this time the weekly had become a daily newspaper. Within the year, I was made shop foreman. Preferring to write, I gave up this position and became a reporter and regional correspondent for the Associated Press. An opening occurred in the leading job printing plant of the town and I was asked to be foreman.

The urge to write was too strong for me to remain content with the mechanics of printing and I persuaded the proprietor to let me launch out on a venture that proved immediately popular—a weekly magazine type of newspaper. Frequently I made notes of editorials and feature articles and then put them into type with my own fingers. Circulation grew, advertising increased, and we were doing so well that I had about given up the idea of going to college.

At a critical moment, W. T. Lowrey, president of Mississippi College, visited our little city on a student recruitment mission. My Sunday school teacher called me and urged me to hear Dr. Lowrey speak. I was impressed by his personality, his scholarly eloquence, his plea for the college and for students. Next day he put it to me squarely that I should go to college immediately or run the risk of never going.

The cashier of the nearby bank, J. C. Ballard, himself a Mississippi College graduate, sent for me and asked what decision I had reached. I told him frankly that I did not have the means to finance a college education. He said: "Go on with what you have. When that gives out, draw on me and you can pay me back from your summer work and after you finish." This clenched the decision. I would go to college!

In the three years' interval between high school graduation and college entrance, two teachers influenced me in opposite directions. The first was the editor under whom I had served my apprenticeship as reporter. He was now semiretired and was employed to write editorials and feature articles for the news-magazine which I edited. He was a skilled writer and taught me much about the art of writing. He had two outstanding characteristics: he loved liquor and hated preachers. Two of his favorite authors were Robert Ingersoll (*Some Mistakes of Moses*) and Thomas Paine *(Age of Reason)*. At least once a month he got drunk and I cared for him over the weekend while he sobered up. His drinking disgusted me but his religious skepticism fascinated me. I began to pride myself on being a "free thinker."

My other out-of-school teacher was the wife of the Baptist pastor, Mrs. I. P. Trotter. She taught a Sunday school class of young men. I enrolled in the class, partly to please my mother and partly because of the teacher's insistence.

She would call every Saturday to remind me to be in Sunday school on Sunday morning. Sometimes she would give me a simple assignment to bring up. Her persistence and interest in me served as something of a foil for the skeptical influence of my atheistic mentor.

The decision to go to Mississippi College was more momentous than I could have possibly realized. An uncle was superintendent of the public schools at Oxford, Mississippi, and, of course, wanted me to attend the University. The push of friends and the pull of President Lowrey prevailed, and so in September, 1904, I found myself on the campus of a college with about three hundred students, an antebellum chapel, some scattered run-down buildings, and a remarkable faculty.

Since I had a year of Latin in high school, I applied to enter the sophomore class. Permission was granted, provided I passed satisfactorily an entrance test. Being a bit rusty, I sought out Professor A. J. Aven (affectionately known as "Ajax") and asked for help in getting ready for the examination. He graciously invited me to his home and coached me for the test. On Sunday he taught a Sunday school class which he urged me to attend. For the first time, I heard the Bible presented in a way that challenged my doubts and objections.

The next semester I entered a college class taught by the venerable H. F. Sproles, whose textbook was E. Y. Mullins' *Why Is Christianity True?*. I re-examined my skeptical position but remained unconvinced.

That spring a campus-wide revival meeting was held under the guidance of P. I. Lipsey, with T. T. Martin as evangelist. Chapel attendance was compulsory; hence, I

listened to the morning sermons but doggedly refused to
go to the evening services—on grounds that I had to study.
My grades were good and I didn't want to risk lowering
them. The truth is that I was afraid I might be convinced
against my will and go over to the "Holy Joes," the ministerial students, some of whom I heartily disliked.

It was Wednesday night and interest in the meeting was
mounting to a climax. An all-night prayer meeting was
held. Somehow I became strangely restless, left my books
and went out on the railroad track behind the boarding-
house, and walked back and forth in the moonlight. I felt
desperately unhappy as with myself I argued the case
against becoming a Christian and resolutely determined
that I was not going to be overpersuaded. What I did not
know was that my name was on the prayer list of those
for whom a devoted band of Christians were at that moment praying.

The next morning in Latin class an unusual thing happened. Professor Aven read the translation, commented on
some of the difficult constructions, then dismissed the class.
As we were leaving, he beckoned me to remain. Together
we went outside and sat on a grassy knoll. Very simply he
told me what Jesus Christ meant to him. He said that he
and others had been praying for me and he felt that my
time had come for decision.

When I began to recite some of my stock objections, he
took out his pocket Testament. He turned to John 7:17,
and read: "If any man will do his will, he shall know of the
doctrine, whether it be of God, or whether I speak of myself."

"It is easy to see that you are not happy in your indecision," he said. "Why not step out on this promise? Here is the scientific test: try it and see. Simply say, 'I will take Christ at his word.' Obey him in a public confession of trust and rest the case on what happens. If he does not fulfil his promise," he continued, "you may go your way in unbelief and I will never bother you again." Holding out his hand, he said, "Will you do it?"

After a silent struggle, I took his hand, and said simply, "I'll try."

In the service that morning, something happened. A strange peace came, my doubts faded, and when the invitation was given I went forward without hesitation and at the close of the meeting was baptized by Dr. Lipsey. A great teacher had made a difference in my life for time and eternity.

Life now took a different turn. I gave up my aloofness, cultivated the friendship of the ministerial students as well as others, and took an interest in something other than books and grades. I was elected editor of the college annual and of the college paper and then made manager of the baseball and football teams.

In the nearby Hillman Institute for young women was a lovely girl, sister-in-law of Dr. Patterson, my former high school teacher. A friendship developed that deepened into love and resulted eventually in my claiming May Riley as my bride.

A year of teaching in a small college followed graduation, with growing interest in church work. One Sunday when I was absent the pastor called the deacons together and, without my knowledge or consent, recommended to the church that I be licensed to preach! I accepted the action as confirmation of my developing sense of "call" and began to cast about for the next steps in preparation.

About that time, Dr. George B. Eager of the faculty of Southern Seminary, Louisville, visited the campus on a student recruitment mission. We talked the matter over and I filled out an application for admission to the seminary. When the session opened in 1909, I found myself enrolled as a student for the ministry. I was led in strange and providential ways into a career that must have been of God's planning, since a few years before this would have been farthest from my thought.

This story is told simply to confirm my thesis that "great teachers are those who make a difference." Consider the life of any Christian who has in some measure been a blessing: begun in helplessness, tempted toward uselessness, guided at strategic moments, shaped by circumstances beyond his own contriving, molded by influences unsought and undeserved, and led toward a destiny unforeseen and undesigned by himself—*the human factor that made the difference was a teacher*. The teacher may or may not have been in a classroom, but at a critical time in the growth process someone as teacher was the human instrumentality divinely used to determine destiny.

He who called himself Teacher and was called Teacher more often than by any other title continues to do that which he began to do and to teach through teachers who have caught his spirit. Stripped to its core, this is education:

> Mark Hopkins sat on one end of a log
> And a farm boy sat on the other.

Mark Hopkins came as a pedagogue.
   And taught as an elder brother.
I don't care what Mark Hopkins taught,
If his Latin was small and his Greek was naught,
For the farm boy he thought, thought he,
   All through the lecture time and quiz,
"The kind of a man I mean to be
   Is the kind of a man Mark Hopkins is."

. . . .

Not all the books on all the shelves,
But what the teachers are, themselves.
For Education is, Making Men;
So is it now, so was it when
Mark Hopkins sat on one end of a log
And James Garfield sat on the other.

ARTHUR GUITERMAN

2

Edgar Young Mullins

Insightful Theologian

> When you read this you can perceive my insight into
> the mystery of Christ. Of this gospel I was made a
> minister according to the gift of God's grace which
> was given me by the working of his power (Eph.
> 3:4,7, RSV).

George H. Betts, for many years distinguished profes·
sor of Bible and religious education at Northwestern Uni·
versity, tells of a lecture by Bishop Vincent, who about one
of his teachers soliloquized: "That old schoolmaster of
mine!—He is dead now—*and I have forgiven him!*—
And I am afraid that was the chronology of the matter." [1]
Some teachers we may not fully forgive even after death
claims them. Some of them we will remember with increasing gratitude to the end of life.

There is an illuminating incident in the Third Gospel
(10:38–42). Martha complained to Jesus because her sister
Mary would not lend a hand with preparation of the meal
but sat listening to the great Teacher.

Mildly rebuking Martha for her anxiety about the meal,
Jesus said concerning Mary, "She has chosen the better
part."

Why the better part? The food would last for perhaps

---

[1] *How to Teach Religion* (New York: The Abingdon Press, 1919),
p. 13.

twenty-four hours; the clothes Martha wore might last twice twenty-four months; the house in which she lived might last twice twenty-four years; the body might last three score years and ten. But what Mary learned at the feet of the Master would last through life and on into eternity. Mary had indeed chosen "the better part."

Is it not for this that the teacher is long remembered? He made his students realize that they did not live by bread alone. He shared with them his insights and himself. He taught more than facts and books—he used *lessons* as a means of teaching *persons*. He somehow imparted confidence that life is good and can be made rich and meaningful. He stirred the smoldering inner fire into a blaze that ever after continued to burn more brightly.

Such was the gift of God to young theologues of Edgar Young Mullins at Southern Seminary in our formative years. We had no need to forgive him for the hard work he demanded of us. In sharing with him in intellectual and spiritual adventure rather than in the prosaic task of memorizing textbooks and lectures, we "chose the better part."

It is not easy to measure the greatness of a teacher. The history of education may record his name as among the illustrious pioneers or creative thinkers; or he may have written books that perpetuate his name and fame; or his activities may have been confined to as small a group as the twelve whom Jesus gathered about him. Perhaps when the books are made up, the name of some humble village pedagogue or Sunday school teacher will head the list.

Baptists have had their share of teachers at all levels— the illustrious, the pioneers, the distinguished authors, as well as the many unheralded and unacclaimed who served in lowly places but left their mark on their generation. Whether great or small, noted or unknown, the distinguishing mark of the effective teacher is much the same: *who he was and what he taught made a difference.*

As I seek to recall the teachers who influenced me most during a more than ordinary period of schooling and then a long lifetime of theological teaching, I am constrained to put at the head of the list Edgar Young Mullins. His story will serve to illustrate my thesis.

Three girls had been born into the home of a Mississippi Baptist pastor and his wife. When the mother placed the fourth arrival in the arms of the father, she proudly announced, "A boy!" The grateful father knelt beside the bed and prayed that the son might become a minister of the gospel.

When Edgar was nine years of age, his parents moved to Texas. The lad grew to manhood, went away to college, and was graduated with honors. He worked for a while as a telegraph operator, then decided to prepare himself to become a lawyer. While attending law school in Dallas, he was converted in a revival meeting held by Major W. E. Penn. With his conversion came his call to be a minister of the gospel.

Returning home, young Mullins told his father and mother of his experience, expecting them to be greatly surprised. His was the surprise when they told him of their prayer of dedication at his birth, and that they had waited in quiet confidence for this answer to their prayer.

Turning aside from law school, Mullins entered Southern Baptist Theological Seminary in 1881. He worked his way through school as manager of the Seminary dining hall.

After four years of study, he was graduated with distinction, recognized as one of the best students in his class.

He served successively as pastor at Harrodsburg, Kentucky; Baltimore, Maryland; and Newton Centre, Massachusetts. At Baltimore he studied in Johns Hopkins University and at Newton Centre continued his studies in Newton Theological Institution (now Andover Newton). These years of pastoral experience and study were highly significant for his future career.

Southern Seminary had passed through a difficult ordeal known as the "Whitsitt controversy." The controversy gathered about an encyclopedia article that Whitsitt, president and teacher of church history at the seminary, had written. He had pointed out that there was no documentary evidence that English Baptists existed prior to 1641. This ran contrary to the Landmark doctrine of "apostolic succession," and stirred up such a storm that Dr. Whitsitt felt constrained to resign.

When the trustees gathered to elect Dr. Whitsitt's successor, Edgar Young Mullins had no intimation of what was happening. A telegram came from the editor of a Kentucky Baptist paper: "Congratulations. Send your photograph. Prestridge."

In her husband's absence on a round of pastoral calls, Mrs. Mullins had opened the telegram. With quick intuition she realized what had happened. When Dr. Mullins reached home, she ran to meet him, crying, "You have been elected president of the Southern Baptist Theological Seminary!" [2]

---

[2] Isla May Mullins, *Edgar Young Mullins, an Intimate Biography* (Nashville: Sunday School Board of SBC, 1929), pp. 106–7.

The presidency carried with it a professorship. Boyce had been professor of theology, Broadus professor of New Testament and homiletics, Whitsitt, professor of church history. To Mullins came the assignment to teach theology. This was his major field of interest and immediately he plunged into the study of theology and philosophy. In the years ahead he was destined to become one of the outstanding thinkers, lecturers, preachers, and writers in this commanding field.

The fiftieth anniversary program (1909) of Southern Seminary featured distinguished men from many parts of the Baptist world. I was asked to cover the meetings. The assignment took me to the office of President Mullins. I can see him now—tall, slim, erect, piercing eyes, neatly trimmed mustache and beard, friendly and approachable, yet with reserve that excluded overfamiliarity. He greeted me cordially and took time to give me the information I needed. He presided over the meetings with that ease and confidence which were later to mark him as a master of assemblies when he served as president of the Southern Baptist Convention and the Baptist World Alliance.

My introduction to Dr. Mullins as teacher was in his systematic theology class. Later I was in his class in biblical theology. When Dr. Mullins took the platform, he almost always lectured. (Never let it be said that one cannot learn from listening to a lecture!) It was my privilege to hear Dr. Mullins' lectures, out of which later grew his volume *The Christian Religion in Its Doctrinal Expression*. His technique was that of stating the point, then illustrating it.

When with characteristic gesture he removed his glasses

and there appeared a twinkle in his eyes, we knew that he was about to give us an illuminating illustration.

I recall his discussion of the difference between freedom and toleration. A horse, hitched to a wagon, is controlled by bit and bridle and reins. He may blink his eyes, shake his head, walk or trot, or even kick or balk. To this extent he is granted a measure of toleration. But he is not free like the unharnessed horse that determines where he shall go. Baptists, Dr. Mullins said, are not content with toleration— they demand full and complete religious liberty.

Dr. Mullins was intensely person-minded. He revolted against the older proof-text method of establishing theological propositions. He was deeply influenced by William James's philosophy of pragmatism and was fascinated by his book *Varieties of Religious Experience.* Here he found his clue to a vital approach to theology. To him the Bible was the inspired record of personal experiences with God, God's dealings with men, and men's experiences with one another. He sought to establish theological truths with human values as the frame of reference.

His *Why Is Christianity True?* introduced a new type of apologetics—the argument for the validity of Christianity from its results in history and in human life. His *Axioms of Religion* undertook to state in the form of axiomatic truths the fundamentals of the Christian faith as it finds expression both in the biblical revelation and in human reaction to this revelation. This brief book lifted him into first place among European and Asian Baptists and was influential in gaining for him the presidency of the Baptist World Alliance.

Dr. Mullins' insight was never more keenly displayed

than in his presentation of the Baptist genius. He departed from the customary polemics of the denominational controversialists and undertook no special pleading for his own religious body. He saw clearly the incompletions of the Reformation theologians, who departed from Roman Catholic doctrine at certain essential points but failed to go all the way with the New Testament and its revealed and logical finality.

At first saying little about the Baptist faith, he enunciated a series of axioms or self-evident truths. These are so true that they neither admit of debate nor need to be established by argument. I recall my excitement and that of my classmates when in a lecture he propounded these axioms:

The theological axiom.—The holy and loving God has a right to be sovereign.

The religious axiom.—All souls have an equal right to direct access to God.

The ecclesiastical axiom.—All believers have a right to equal privileges in the church.

The moral axiom.—To be responsible, man must be free.

The religio-civic axiom.—A free church in a free state.

The social axiom.—Love your neighbor as yourself.[3]

At once we saw what we had believed all along—that any body of Christians that followed the New Testament would have to agree with these self-evident statements and that it was the Baptist heritage and stewardship to have embodied these truths and accepted the obligation to share them. We saw that our mission was, not to fight

---

[3] E. Y. Mullins, *The Axioms of Religion* (Philadelphia: American Baptist Publication Society, 1908), pp. 73–74.

for "Baptist doctrines" as sectarians nor against other Christians with a different or even conflicting brand of doctrine, but so to illuminate the self-evident truth as to get it accepted and obeyed by all who sought it sincerely.

Dr. Mullins possessed in rare degree the quality which we speak of as "insight." There are two obvious ways of arriving at truth. One is by the process of research, analysis and synthesis, and of painstaking observation and experimentation. The other is by insight, the quick intuitive perception of truth that lies beyond and above the plodding search of the investigator. The two processes are not incompatible. A moment of insight may mean years of research for verification; and the long pathway of research may suddenly be rewarded by the flash of insight that illuminates the pathway of the tedious climb. The truly creative thinker and teacher is the one who combines both processes and is at once the pragmatist and the idealist.

Dr. Mullins was thoroughly practical, the exact scholar, the careful researcher. This quality was matched by his perceptiveness, his rhythm of thought that dealt now with the practical, now with the ideal. He was a master of details. The word "mastery" was often on his lips. We could not conceive his doing anything in slipshod fashion and a student who turned in slovenly work felt the lash of his criticism. He was a master administrator and as such achieved notable results. He dealt with small details with the same scrupulous care he gave to momentous issues.

Insightfulness was seen in Dr. Mullins' keen and clear moral discernment. In facing a moral problem, he sought solution by reference to a basic moral principle. One frame of reference was the sovereign will of God, which he conceived to be an expression of the holy nature of God. "God acts righteously because he is righteous," he would say. Submitting a question to this test, he would cut through nonessentials and fallacies and come straight to the heart of the matter with the question, "What is right according to the nature and the will of God?" He differed with Augustine and Calvin at a number of points but followed them closely in their doctrine of the sovereignty of God. His touchstone was, "The sovereign God has the right to rule."

Again, his insight expressed itself in his concept of the inviolable rights of the individual in society. In philosophy and psychology, he was a personalist. His fundamental ethical principle was respect for personality.

When asked what distinctive Baptist principle was central, about which the others gathered, he stated his axiom: "All men have an equal right to direct access to God." Violation of this principle brought Christianity into a long eclipse. In the hierarchical system that developed, direct relation to God was lost: forgiveness became absolution; prayer became confession to a priest; regeneration was effected by baptism administered preferably in infancy; the implanted life was sustained by penance and the mass; all risk of final damnation was removed by extreme unction; purgatory cleansed the soul and guaranteed eventual entrance into heaven. "The whole machinery of religion passes over into the hands of a human priesthood with its terrible power of spiritual tyranny." Poles apart from this perverted system, Dr. Mullins showed, stand those who hold simply that "all souls have an equal right to access to God." [4]

---

[4] *Op. cit.*, p. 104.

Dr. Mullins was frequently attacked on the ground of his unorthodoxy. Here again his insight into biblical truth prevailed. In the controversy over evolution, when some tried to make one's position on this subject a test of faith and fellowship, Dr. Mullins held simply that truth is unitary and cannot contradict itself. Whatever scientists discover to be fact in the physical realm would be found consonant with truth in the spiritual realm. Consistently he posed the question, "What are the facts?" He deftly showed that Christianity has nothing to fear from scientific discovery.

When the dust of controversy had settled, Dr. Mullins knew that right and truth would prevail. He was not careful to be with the popular majority. His concern was to be right and then to bring the majority to the side of right. In his writings and in his lectures he stated the Baptist position with such clarity and convincingness that even those who opposed him were inclined to agree with him.

Dr. Mullins' insight was displayed in his foresight of trends that would lead Southern Baptists into an expansion that would make them the leading free church denomination in America.

This trend would be away from convention control toward local church development; away from controversy toward co-operation; away from a pulpit-centered ministry toward a well-rounded pastoral ministry; away from a church that made churchgoing and listening central toward a church that enlisted its local membership in worship, teaching, and training—with diminishing distinction between the clergy and the laity. Dr. Mullins took a leading part in the International Sunday School Association, saving it from disaster when, during the period of controversy, the Sunday school movement was in danger of being divorced from denominational control. He was intensely missionary in spirit and passionately devoted to evangelism. He held many revival meetings and was an effective personal soul-winner. He served as chaplain in World War II and was in great demand as preacher in the camps at home and with men overseas.

In a remarkable way, he combined theological scholarship with practical effectiveness denominationally, interdenominationally, and internationally. He was God's gift to Southern Baptists at a time when they might have been tempted to narrowness and provincialism. He led them in the movement to make their churches effective instruments of Christ's redemptive purpose through teaching, preaching, and healing. It was through his insight and foresight that Southern Seminary established the first credit course in religious education and the first full department of missions in an American seminary.

In his leadership of the Baptist World Alliance (president 1923–28), Dr. Mullins was pre-eminently the insightful theologian-teacher. Europe had just emerged from World War I, in which the United States had played a strategic part and had achieved international hegemony. The war had been fought "to make the world safe for democracy," but this safety was threatened by reprisals, deepseated national hatreds, insecure religious foundations, and near moral chaos. The Baptist message and mission needed restatement and reinterpretation in terms of worldwide political, social, and spiritual rebuilding. The strong, clear voice of Mullins became the Baptist voice that rallied scattered and disorganized bodies throughout Europe. His strong restatement of the Baptist faith and mission brought renewed conviction and enthusiasm for world responsibility and opportunity at one of the great turning points in Western history.

Dr. Mullins suffered a stroke in June, 1928, from which he died in November. The World Congress met in Toronto, Canada, in July. When it became evident that Dr. Mullins could not attend and preside, he called and asked that I take the manuscript of his presidential address and deliver it to Dr. George W. Truett, who read it to the Congress. It was a sad but exalted occasion when the eloquent preacher Truett spoke the words written by the master theologian Mullins. The address was titled "Baptist Life in the World's Life." Rarely have I seen an audience so profoundly moved.

The psalmist prayed, "Establish thou the work of our hands upon us; yea, the work of our hands establish thou it" (90:17). This, after all, is the supreme test: Does a man's work abide? It will abide only as it is done under the will of God for the purposes of Jesus Christ, and as it is built upon the foundation of imperishable Christian character.

Death does not bring to an end the career of a man whose work has fulfilled these requirements. And so Dr. Mullins lives on, in the tender memories of loved ones and intimate friends; in the gratitude of countless students into whose lives he invested his life; in the appreciation of his denomination and of Christian men and women of every name; in the record of his splendid achievements for the cause of Christ.

On Dr. Mullins' desk was a simple, framed card, which caught his eye whenever he looked up from his work. It contained just three words: "Thy Kingdom Come." This was his supreme ambition—to have a worthy part in bringing in the kingdom of God. This is his legacy—that the kingdom is nearer to earth than it otherwise would have been had he not lived. In the years that lie ahead God will no doubt establish more and more the work of his hands, and make us to realize even more than we do now the significance of the inscription on his monument, taken from John Bunyan:

> My sword I give to him who shall succeed me;
> My courage and skill to him that can get it,
> My marks and scars I carry with me
> To be a witness for me that I have fought
>   his battles
> Who will now be my rewarder.

"And so he passed over, and all the trumpets sounded on the other side." [5]

---

[5] Isla May Mullins, *op. cit.*, p. 217.

3
John Richard Sampey
Statesman-Scholar

He gives power to the faint,
    and to him who has no might he
    increases strength.
Even youths shall faint and be
      weary,
    and young men shall fall exhausted;
but they who wait for the Lord
    shall renew their strength,
    they shall mount up with wings
      like eagles,
they shall run and not be weary,
    they shall walk and not faint.
ISAIAH 40:29–31, RSV

His students affectionately called him "Tiglath-pileser." Somehow he reminded them of Pul, the Assyrian warrior-king who is reputed to have conquered forty-two nations.

Dr. Sampey was not a warlike man but he was a student of military science and to the end of his life was an unreconstructed rebel. He was a tremendous admirer of Robert E. Lee, who was his greatest hero after the apostle Paul.

John Richard Sampey was born in Fort Deposit, Alabama, September 27, 1863. Like Edgar Young Mullins, his contemporary and colleague, he was born in a minister's home. His father was a Methodist minister but was led through prayer and Bible study to become a Baptist. Soon after the baby's birth, the family moved from Fort Deposit to Ramer, Alabama. He lived the uneventful life of a village preacher's son, attending Sunday school and listening regularly to his father's sermons.

His conversion occurred when he was thirteen years old. Earlier he had realized that he needed a Saviour but no one seemed to be interested in his religious condition, not even his father. At thirteen, during a revival meeting, he became deeply convicted of his sin. I, along with others, was moved to tears by his simple recital of his salvation experience:

In the next two years or more I did not get nearer to God. I learned to use profane language and fell into other sins. Sometimes I would pray for forgiveness; and I read the Bible and attended preaching services. I thought that before I could be saved I must have some notable experience like that of Saul on the road to Damascus. At times I thought I was getting better, and at other times it seemed that I was becoming more wicked. I had no peace in my heart. The burden of my sins I could not shake off, and no one told me just what I needed to do to get rid of the burden. I was floundering in the slough of despond.

As I lay on the trundle bed on the night of March 3, 1877, I could not go to sleep. We had just had family prayers. Father was reading and Mother was knitting. My younger brother had fallen asleep beside me; but I was in distress over my sins. In my desperation I lifted my eyes upward and began to talk in a whisper to the Saviour. I said to him: "Lord Jesus, I do not know what to do. I have prayed, but I get no relief. I have read the Bible, but my sins are still a burden on my soul. I have listened to preaching, but find no help. I do not know what to do except to turn it all over to you; and if I am lost, I will go down trusting you!"

Then something happened. It seemed that a great Presence filled the room and said to me almost in audible words: "My boy, I have been waiting for you to do what you have just done. You can count on me to save you. I will not fail you." My pillow was presently wet with tears of joy that Christ Jesus was now my personal Saviour. I looked up to the old family clock on the mantel, and it was five minutes to eight o'clock on the evening of March 3, 1877, the day before Rutherford B. Hayes was inaugurated as President of the United States. . . .

I did not at first tell anyone of my conversion. I kept the secret from March until July. On Saturday before the second Sunday in July, 1877, I stepped forward and gave Pastor B. A. Jackson my hand when he opened the doors of the church after the close of his sermon. I might have been waiting for the annual protracted meeting in August, but the urge to declare my faith publicly was so great that I could wait no longer.

I was asked to tell my Christian experience, and I did so. I remember that Pastor Jackson asked me how I felt toward Christian people, and I told him that I had always liked to be with them and hear them talk, but that lately I seemed to love them more than ever. He turned to the church members and said, "Hereby we know that we have passed from death unto life, because we love the brethren." I rejoice that this mark of a Christian has been with me through all the years that have followed. I love everybody who loves my Saviour.[1]

Two years after his baptism, the fifteen-year-old boy was made superintendent of the Sunday school. A year later, without his having requested it, the church licensed him to preach. With unconcealed emotion, Dr. Sampey told of the sacrifices of his father and mother in order that he might go to college. He was scarcely twenty years of age when

---

[1] John R. Sampey, *Memoirs* (Nashville: Broadman Press, 1947), pp. 6–7.

he was graduated from Howard College with highest honors of his class.

Entering Southern Seminary, Louisville, Kentucky, immediately following college graduation, young Sampey came under the influence of the great teachers of that institution, notably James P. Boyce and John A. Broadus. Broadus was at the height of his powers as teacher, as preacher, and as denominational leader. His influence on young Sampey, as on all of his students, was transforming.

In later years, Dr. Sampey delighted to tell stories of Dr. Broadus, whom he considered the greatest teacher and preacher he had ever known.

The early struggles of Southern Seminary for survival constitute a saga worthy of the pen of an epic poet. Dr. Sampey often told with great emotion the story of the founding of the seminary in 1859 by the "Big Four"—Boyce, Broadus, Manly, and Williams. When five years later the South lay prostrate after the tragic War Between the States, the four men met to see what could be done to revive the seminary, which had been closed during the latter part of the war. Dr. Boyce pointed out that the school, which had so hopeful a beginning, did not have a very strong hold on the confidence and affections of Baptists in several states. If the school were abandoned, a whole generation or more would elapse, and those present would be in their graves before brethren would have the heart to attempt again the establishment of a theological school. "We had prayed over the question, again and again," Dr. Boyce recorded. "Presently someone said, 'Suppose we quietly agree that the Seminary may die, but we'll die first.' All heads were silently bowed and the matter was decided." [2]

On the death of Dr. Boyce, Dr. Broadus became president of the seminary. Two brilliant students had received appointment as assistant professors, John R. Sampey and A. T. Robertson. Dr. Sampey was offered his choice of Old Testament or New Testament. He replied: "As much as I love New Testament and Greek, Robertson is my superior in this field. I will therefore take Old Testament and Hebrew and suggest that Robertson be given New Testament and Greek."

This was a momentous decision. With great zeal Dr. Sampey threw himself into the task of mastering the Old Testament and especially the Hebrew language. Summer courses in Hebrew were being offered by the renowned William Rainey Harper at Yale University. Dr. Sampey attended these courses and returned to his teaching with a tremendous enthusiasm for Hebrew.

Of French descent, Dr. Sampey possessed innately the vivacity and drive characteristic of the Frenchman. With him, Hebrew was "no dead language," but came alive as he made Old Testament history and characters live and breathe before his students. To a student who plodded painfully and prosaicly through a translation of Isaiah, he would say, "Wait a minute! Start over now! Stick your head in the air, get your tail over the dashboard, snort once or twice, and go down the pike!" To a student who objected that he saw no use in learning Hebrew, he said, "You'll

---

[2] John A. Broadus, *Memoirs of James P. Boyce* (New York: A. C. Armstrong & Son, 1893), p. 200.

have to learn Hebrew, if you want to talk to the saints in heaven."

I had junior Hebrew under professor W. J. McGlothlin, whose major field was church history. Dr. McGlothlin taught Hebrew because he had to, not because he wanted to. I developed a keen distaste for the class. But the next year, when I had senior Hebrew under Dr. Sampey, my whole attitude changed. There was no less work, for he drilled us as if we were a company of soldiers getting ready for battle. There was never a dull moment in his classes. One morning I was translating from Jonah: "Jonah was in the *stomach* of the fish three days and three nights." Dr. Sampey interrupted, "Belly, Brother Dobbins, belly— don't be so squeamish."

Year after year Dr. Sampey brought a series of chapel talks on Lee during the week when the General's birthday was celebrated. This afforded him opportunity not only to tell of his hero but to give the South's side of the story in "the War Between the States" (never "the Civil War"). We relived the bloody battles and felt the heartbreak of Lee and his lieutenants as defeat closed in on the Confederacy and the surrender at Appomatox became inevitable. Then we saw the South rise from the ashes of disaster under the leadership of Lee, the statesman and educator, who helped to guide the broken land to a new era of recovery and prosperity.

"Robert E. Lee," Dr. Sampey said one day in class, "was the greatest man American history records."

"Do you think he was any greater than Ulysses S. Grant?" a northern student asked.

With biting sarcasm Dr. Sampey trimmed him down,

then apologized for losing his temper. "But you mightily provoked me," he vindicated himself. "When you asked that question, Sir, you drapped your 'lasses jug." Dr. Sampey remained an unreconstructed rebel. He was twenty-one years old, he once remarked, before he knew that "damyankee" was two words.

In English Old Testament class he made Moses and David and the prophets and the kings and generals march across the stage of history with the vividness of a motion picture, yet with such accuracy of detail as to be our admiration and despair.

Many seminary professors, because they loved to preach and had the shepherd heart, were pastors of nearby rural churches. Dr. Sampey's country church was his pride and joy. In his *Memoirs* he tells of many happy experiences as he served the church and led in revival meetings. Pastoral counseling in its modern guise had not appeared, but Dr. Sampey was an effective "counselor" to members of his flock. He did not engage in chit-chat but went directly to the heart of things. In making his rounds of pastoral calls, to a deacon he might say, "I understand that you got drunk two weeks ago. Let's get at the heart of it so that it will never happen again."

"How can I overcome my dreadful drink habit?" he was asked.

"When you feel the temptation of thirst for a drink, just drop down on your knees wherever you are and ask Christ Jesus to help you. Rest assured that he will."

Visiting a husband and wife in marital difficulty, he might say, "Tell me all about it—don't hold anything back. Then before I go I want to see you kiss and make up."

He studied the names on the church roll—resident and nonresident, active and backslidden. When in this study the church clerk turned over to him the membership roll, Dr. Sampey noted that after certain names were the initials, "N.C." Puzzled, he inquired as to whether these members had removed to North Carolina. "Of course not," the clerk replied. "Don't you know what N.C. stands for? It means no 'count."

Enlisting the aid of deacons and deaconesses (Dr. Sampey was firmly convinced that the New Testament justified the office of deaconess), he instituted the practice of an annual spiritual inventory, seeking to "grade" each member on the quality of his spiritual and moral life. He delighted to tell that after the first inventory disclosed an average grade of 74, the next showed a grade of 79, and so progressively upward. To him, the beloved Forks of Elkhorn Church was a laboratory for the winning and development of Christians, not just a preaching place nor a means of supplementing a meager salary.

The election of Dr. Sampey to succeed President Mullins took him out of the classroom and his country pastorate and plunged him into a sea of difficulties and denominational responsibilities. The seminary had removed from its overcrowded downtown quarters to its spacious suburban campus. President Mullins had led in the campaign for a two million-dollar building fund. He died in 1928; the financial crash came in 1929. Unpaid subscriptions were not worth the paper they were written on. Dr. Sampey found himself faced with a debt of nine hundred thousand dollars and no money with which to pay even the interest. I was drafted to be treasurer (without pay) and we immediately began a drastic program of economy. Expenses and salaries were cut to the bone but there was never a murmur of complaint.

Few of this generation realize the distress of those depression years. Vividly I recall the meeting of the Executive Committee of the Convention in 1933 at Nashville. Report after report of the Convention's boards and agencies indicated practical bankruptcy. At length Dr. L. R. Scarborough, president of Southwestern Seminary, arose and choking with emotion said in effect, "Brethren, we are through at Southwestern. For two years we haven't paid faculty salaries. We have nothing with which to meet expenses. Our percentage of the allocation will not see us through another year. Here is my resignation and I turn over to you the seminary property. You'll have to sell it to pay our debts, and Southwestern will go out of existence."

There was a stunned silence. We sat in tears. Then Dr. Sampey arose, drummed with his fingers on the table in characteristic fashion, and said in effect, "I may lose my job for what I am about to say. Southern Seminary has some income from endowment on which we can live. I move that Southern Seminary's apportionment be cut and the difference given to Southwestern."

This turned the tide for Southwestern, gave it a new lease on life, and under God made possible its marvelous history of growth and achievement.

Dr. Sampey was a unique and highly effective evangelist. His favorite method was to preach through the high spots of one or more books of the Bible—Isaiah the first week and Matthew, Mark, or Luke the second; or the Gospel of John the first week and Acts the second.

Having preached to the arousing of conviction of sin, he would say: "Come forward and say to me whatever the Holy Spirit prompts you to say, whether to ask for membership in the church, or to confess your sins, or to avow some noble life purpose." And they came down by the hundreds confessing their sins and avowing their intention, as the preacher put it, to "surrender all the keys to the Lord Jesus." He found that when church members got right, sinners were saved. No matter whether the text was in the Old Testament or the New, it always led to the need of a Saviour from sin and the grace of God in Christ bestowing forgiveness and bringing new life and fruitfulness.

During the crucial prewar years the ecumenical movement began to take shape. Dr. Sampey was intensely interested in this movement toward greater Christian unity. He was no ecumenic, but he believed that evangelical Christian bodies should think of themselves as allies rather than as enemies. Missionary journeys to Brazil, Japan, China, and the Middle East had intensified his concern for worldwide advance in the missionary enterprise.

In 1935, Dr. Sampey was elected president of the Southern Baptist Convention. He urged the importance of having a representative of the Convention in both the Conference on Life and Work in Oxford and the Conference on Faith and Order in Edinburgh. Promptly the Convention authorized him to go as its representative. His speech in the plenary session on "The Church of the New Testament" made a profound impression.

In these ecumenical meetings Dr. Sampey found himself in the midst of clergymen dressed in a variety of vestments. He himself wore his usual street clothes. It is told that an effeminate little priest looked up at Dr. Sampey curiously and asked, "To which one of the sects do you belong?"

"To the male sex!" Dr. Sampey snapped in reply. "To what sex do you belong?"

Dr. Sampey was no less a Baptist—and Southern Baptist—because of his broad sympathies. When the one hundredth anniversary of the Southern Baptist Convention was being celebrated in 1945, I interviewed Dr. Sampey. "In your opinion, what will be the growth of Southern Baptists in the hundred years ahead?"

Using a pencil and the back of an envelope, he made some quick calculations. "Within twenty years (1965) we should have passed the ten million mark in membership, and by 2045 we should be at least fifty million strong."

Concerning Baptists as a whole, looking back to 1905 (the organization of the Baptist World Alliance), when there were approximately six million Baptists in the world, and to their increase to approximately sixteen million in 1945, he forecast a total Baptist constituency by 2045 of one hundred million. "Of course this growth," he said, "is predicated on two assumptions: that we remain faithful to our position concerning the lordship of Jesus Christ and the divine authority of the Bible, and our continued and intensified devotion to evangelism and missions."

Toward the last, Dr. Sampey developed a heart murmur which slowed him down. He resigned the seminary presidency in 1942, at the ripe age of 79. Dr. Ellis A. Fuller, pastor of the great First Church of Atlanta, was elected to succeed him. It was a dramatic moment when Dr. Sampey, just before leading the inaugural prayer, took off his beloved Brazilian cape and put it on the shoulders of the new

president, with the prayer that Elisha made to Elijah—
that he be given a double portion of the prophet's blessing.

Dr. Sampey continued in full mental vigor through the
remaining seven years of his retirement. Sometimes, in the
absence of the professor, he would teach the senior Hebrew
class, much to the joy of the students. Occasionally he
would attend faculty meetings. Once when we were solic-
itously inquiring about his health, he said, "My doctor has
given me a clean bill of health except for this heart murmur. Really, my only trouble is that when I sit down for
awhile, my feet swell and grow numb." Then, with a twinkle in his eye, he remarked, "I thank God that it has begun
at that end!"

When asked, "What do you consider your greatest lifework?" Dr. Sampey passed in review some of his accom-
plishments and honors. Then he said, "I count my greatest
work to have been chairman of the Uniform Lessons Committee of the International Sunday School Association
(later the International Council of Religious Education)
for forty-six years." He was the great champion of a Bible-
centered curriculum for the Sunday schools of the world
during these critical years. More than any other one man
he gave guidance to the selection of the lesson cycles
during almost half a century.

Those of us who heard him will never forget his closing
address to the seminary graduates. His theme was: "Give
Christ Jesus All the Keys." He concluded: "Men, my
brothers, there is no work comparable to the preaching of
the gospel to lost men. Christ Jesus expects of each of us
that we shall witness for him. He would say to each of us
just what he said to the healed demoniac, 'Go, tell.' Tell

what great things the Lord has done for you. The world will listen to such a story. There is nothing the world needs more than the story of our deliverance through Christ. Tell it wherever you go. Let the good news fill all lands, even in spite of wars. Men are dying without Christ. Go, tell!"

By the test, "Did he make a difference?" John R. Sampey rates high as a great teacher. He was more than classroom master—almost everything he did had teaching value. More than it can ever know, the present generation of Baptists is indebted to this man who left an indelible impress on the denomination of his day as he broadened its outlook, led it to share constructively with Christians of other names, and helped to keep it Bible-centered and Christ-mastered.

His call comes ringing down to us through the years: "Give Christ Jesus all the keys!"

4
Archibald Thomas Robertson
Prodigious Author

For to me to live is Christ, and to die is gain (Phil. 1:21).

It was my first day of classes at Southern Seminary. Along with eighty other students, I had handed in my enrolment card. Seated at the desk with me was J. L. Green of Mississippi. The class was New Testament Survey. The professor picked out a card, peered at us, then announced: "Brother Green will please recite."

Green, scared almost stiff, half arose and hesitatingly said, "Professor, there are two Greens here. Which one are you calling on?"

The professor looked at him quizzically for a moment, then said, "You look green enough, you'll do. What is the title of the first chapter of my Jesus book?"

Green didn't even know there was such a book. He sat down in dismay as the professor wrote an obvious zero on the card. Warning that no one should ever come to his class unprepared, he went down the line until a fortunate student could give the right answer.

This was my introduction to A. T. Robertson, known as "Dr. Bob" by seniors and graduate students, but held in awe (almost terror) by first-year men. A student might be excused from recitation if he handed in a note stating the reason for his inability; otherwise, he was held strictly to account. He assumed that a student was in the seminary for one reason—to bring up the assignments. We soon learned that failure to do this brought severe consequences.

Archibald Thomas Robertson was born November 6, 1863, at Cherbury, Virginia. Here he spent the first twelve years of his life, after which the family moved to North Carolina. His boyhood and youth were spent in reconstruction days when the South lay prostrate. His parents knew the strain of poverty and only by stint of great sacrifice, the help of friends, and his own labor did young Robertson get his college education at Wake Forest. With ten dollars borrowed from a neighbor for his railroad ticket, he arrived at Wake Forest with $2.50 in his pocket. Six years later he left with his A.B. degree and the highest honors of any man of his class.

Greek language and literature fascinated him. By college graduation, he had read Homer, Xenophen, Thucydides, Herodotus, Aeschylus, Euripides, Demosthenes, Lysias, Plato, and some of the plays of Aristophanes. He was inspired by, and the inspiration of, his great professor, Dr. W. B. Royall.

When young Robertson entered Southern Seminary, Dr. Broadus immediately spotted him as a Greek scholar. He was exempted from junior Greek and, of course, led his class in senior Greek. On completion of his seminary courses, he was appointed assistant to Dr. Broadus in New Testament and homiletics.

Dr. Robertson became the outstanding New Testament Greek scholar of his era. He was the most nearly authentic genius I have ever known. Yet he would have disdainfully rejected such a designation.

Euphonious title, conceived by a shirk,
Distressed by the harsh monosyllable, work.

The New Testament, whether in English or in Greek,
was to Dr. Robertson a means to an end. The end was to
make Jesus Christ known, loved, obeyed. He took God in
Christ seriously. He was interested in criticism and was a
master of the critical apparatus, but his concern was to get
back as nearly as possible to the original meaning of the
inspired writers of the New Testament. There were times
in his classroom when it almost seemed that Jesus himself
was present, that the events of his early life were being re-
enacted, and that we who took part in lecture and in dialogue were back in the first century as witnesses of what
transpired. We often remarked that it was worth the price
of an admission ticket to be in his New Testament survey
class.

A part of Dr. Robertson's fascination was his grim sense
of humor. His sarcasm at times was like a Damascus blade.
It was said that he could cut off the head of a student with
such a keen stroke that he would not know it until he
sneezed the next day! This was an element of his sense of
mission in teaching—to take the conceit out of students
who thought more highly of themselves than they ought
to think.

I was driving him to the railroad station one day when
he turned and asked, "Dobbins, the first-year students
don't like me, do they?" I tried to hedge, but he continued,
"Broadus was a past master at puncturing the conceit of
bigheaded young preachers. He passed on to me this responsibility and I am simply trying to fulfil it." Yet in times

of distress he was the student's unfailing friend, with a heart as tender as a woman's.

Some of his sayings became proverbial. For example:

"The best proof of the inspiration of the Bible is that it has stood so much bad preaching."

"It's a mighty poor pastor who never has any trouble."

"The chief end of some men is to glorify God and annoy him forever."

To a student who claimed divine inspiration, Dr. Robertson said, "Well, God speaks in different ways to man; once he spoke to a donkey."

"Sanctified," he said, "means cleansed. I'd rather have a clean gourd and fresh water than a gold cup with fly specks." To a student who came to him to complain because he had failed the examination, Dr. Robertson said, "Excuse me, Brother, but all I can do for you is pray for you—and flunk you."

I chanced to be walking across the campus with him on the occasion of his sixtieth birthday. He remarked that he had just finished reading the Greek New Testament for the thirtieth time. "Is there anything left for you to learn?" I asked.

"I never read for five minutes," he replied, "that I do not find something new."

"Writing maketh a full man," said Bacon. But it takes a full man to write anything of much consequence. Dr. Robertson waited nearly twenty years before he began his great career as author. Then book after book poured from his pen until the volumes numbered forty-five: *Word Pictures* (6 vols.), four grammars, fourteen commentaries, eleven histories, ten character studies. His books possess a simplicity and charm of style that often conceal the depth of his scholarship, especially his popular works. His *magnum opus* is, of course, his *Grammar of the Greek New Testament in the Light of Historical Research.* He was twenty-six years in the writing of his masterpiece of nearly fifteen hundred pages, which stands as the most authoritative work of its kind in the field. We were told in Rome that it is the standard reference text in the Vatican. His *Word Pictures* (in six volumes) covers every book of the New Testament and is perhaps referred to by preachers and by lesson writers more than any other single commentary.

Dr. Robertson traveled widely and was greatly honored throughout the Baptist world in his latter years. Dr. R. H. Pitt, editor of the Virginia *Religious Herald,* was the first to suggest a world organization of Baptists (1895). His editorial, however, went almost unnoticed. Nine years later Dr. Robertson wrote an unsigned editorial for the *Baptist Argus,* entitled "Why Not a Baptist World Congress?" The appeal met with prompt response on both sides of the Atlantic and one year later (1905) the first Baptist World Congress was held in London, England. More than to any other man, this great organization owes its origin to A. T. Robertson.

What was the secret of Dr. Robertson's prodigious authorship?

First, he had something to say. Jesus Christ possessed him, filled his horizon, challenged him to explore the incalculable riches of the gospel, demanded of him that he share to the utmost what had been entrusted to him as too precious to keep. Second, he knew how to budget his time. His afternoons he kept sacred for study and writing. Nothing but emergencies were allowed to interfere with his schedule. Third, he put himself under discipline. Thoroughness was the mark of all that he did. He abhorred slipshodness in himself or in another. Fourth, he combined work with prayer. He lived in the atmosphere of prayer and work and made no sharp distinction between the two. I never heard him pray a long prayer. He was sensitive to cold and I can hear him now as he opened the class with prayer: "Lord, help us today in our work (somebody close that window!) for Jesus sake, Amen." Fifth, he was convinced that writing is the most effective way by which a teacher or preacher can extend his ministry beyond his classroom or pulpit and beyond the limits of his earthly life.

The young seminarian who was to become renowned as scholar and teacher did not come by his mastery easily. Dr. Broadus is said to have spoken of him as having "a weakness for doing everything thoroughly." When he was appointed to a professorship on the faculty, he wrote in his diary, "No one feels so much as I my utter unfitness for the position." Later he wrote, "I am sure I do not know how to teach, but I am equally determined, by the grace of God, to learn how." He reached a low point in self-depreciation when he wrote, "I am a poor worthless worm as I never saw myself before."

A turning point came when he wrote, "I need a wife to cheer me up." Not long after, he found such a wife in his great teacher's charming daughter, Ella Broadus. Brilliant in her own right, a devoted wife and mother, a charming hostess, a wise counselor of student wives, a devout Christian and churchwoman, she completely filled the emptiness in his former life. The Robertsons were our close neighbors through the years and Mrs. Robertson was as a mother to my wife.

The budding teacher realized that proficiency in Greek was not enough. In addition to Latin, which he already knew, he must learn Sanskrit, German, and French. A year abroad, on leave of absence, gave him this coveted opportunity.

Dr. Robertson did not achieve his reputation as teacher because of skill as a classroom technician. It is doubtful if he ever gave attention to books on methodology. His distinction stemmed from his massive intellect, his mastery of the subject, his vividness of portrayal, his understanding of human nature, his spontaneous humor, and, above all, his devotion to Jesus Christ. When he seemed to be severe, it was for the student's good, not for satisfying his own ego; when his sarcasm bit into a student, it was because he detected insincerity, against which he revolted with a positive repugnance for anything resembling sham.

Dr. Robertson entered the era of national and international acclaim as popular lecturer in 1911, when he was invited to be the featured speaker at Northfield, Massachusetts. It was here that D. L. Moody brought together each year notables from many parts of the world for conference and inspiration. Bible lecturers were supposed to be scholarly. Therefore, they were ponderous and often dull. Robertson brought something new and different— profound scholarship illuminated by pathos and simple eloquence, wit and humor, quizzical thrusts and stimulation to thinking and heart-searching. In it all was a naturalness and unaffectedness that disarmed his would-be critics.

Scholars were long puzzled by the Greek of the New Testament. According to classical standards and grammar, there were glaring faults of idiom and construction. Since it could not be accepted that the Holy Spirit would inspire men to write bad Greek, a generally held theory was that the language of the New Testament was "Holy Spirit Greek," an assumption justified by the right of the Divine Inspirer to use any kind of Greek he pleased. Then came the revolutionary discoveries of first-century papyri and the work of Adolph Deissman in the translation of manuscripts reflecting Greek usage of that era. The startling truth then appeared. The New Testament was written in the *koine* (common language) of the day and was perfectly good Greek, judged by this standard.

The study of the Greek New Testament in the light of historical research became to Dr. Robertson a "magnificent obsession." The Gospels, the Epistles, and the Revelation became human documents throbbing with life, all the more clearly inspired because of the Holy Spirit's use of human instrumentality. He became independent of tradition and broke through encrusted translations and theories of revelation and inspiration to the vital messages of the writers not only for their day but also for ours. Due to his searching study, "new light broke through from the old book." An era of revisions and translations into modern speech emerged. Almost all modern translators acknowledge their indebtedness to A. T. Robertson.

As Dr. Robertson's fame spread, he came to be in wide demand as a lecturer. With his worn Greek New Testament in hand, he stood before audiences large and small, at home and abroad, and captivated his listeners with his fresh, dynamic, dramatic expositions. His humor was of the spontaneous kind, somewhat like that of Will Rogers, and gave cutting edge to his interpretations.

I think he was the least concerned about popularity and public opinion of any great teacher I ever knew. His wife said that it offended him almost to the point of disgust when, after a lecture, there were those who tried to lionize him. Jesus Christ filled his horizon. I have heard him say that he could go along with a man who differed from him at many points, but they parted company if suspicion were thrown on the divinity or lordship or saviourhood of Jesus Christ. He declared that the center about which Paul's great life revolved is the Philippians confession: "For to me to live is Christ, and to die is gain" (1:21). This may well be taken as the keynote of Dr. Robertson's life and the secret of his prodigious labors.

Four days a week Dr. Robertson taught alternately an eight o'clock Greek class and a nine-thirty class in English New Testament, with a senior Greek class on Monday afternoon. His other daytime hours were spent in his study in ceaseless reading and writing. He never took work home with him at night. His evenings were reserved for his family. In his home he was a model of considerateness and an ideal host to the many friends and students with whom he and his wife shared their hospitality.

Never shall I forget the afternoon of September 24, 1934. About half through his Greek class, Dr. Robertson said, "I don't feel well. I shall have to dismiss the class." Professor Hersey Davis took his beloved teacher and colleague to his home, about a half block from ours.

Returning from my office, I was met by my wife, running

and out of breath. "Hurry! Hurry!" she cried, "Something has happened to Dr. Robertson."

I ran and Mrs. Robertson met me at the door. There was a look of unutterable anguish on her face. She took my outstretched hand in both of hers, and whispered, "He's gone, he's gone."

I tried as best I could to comfort her, then hurried home to telephone Dr. Sampey. He afterward told me that when I broke the news, pain went through his heart from which he never recovered.

Funeral services were held in his beloved Fourth Avenue Church. Faculty, students, and friends filled the auditorium to overflowing. The pastor, Dr. A. R. Christie, presided and spoke briefly on behalf of the church. Dr. John R. Cunningham, president of Presbyterian Theological Seminary, brought a tribute on behalf of the Christian community. Dr. John R. Sampey told of his contribution to the seminary, to Baptists, and to the Christian world. With a wave of his hand toward the flower-covered coffin, Dr. Sampey said, "Farewell, dear friend! auf Wiedersehen." The service closed with Dr. Robertson's favorite hymn:

> O could I speak the matchless worth,
> O could I sound the glories forth
> Which in my Saviour shine,
> I'd soar and touch the heavenly strings
> And vie with Gabriel while he sings
> In notes almost divine.

Often have my wife and I visited Cave Hill cemetery, where lie many whom we have loved and lost for awhile. Dr. Robertson's grave marker is a granite cross, with the inscription: "To me to live is Christ, and to die is gain."

5

Charles Spurgeon Gardner

Conscience-Quickener

> Thus, sinning against your brethren and wounding
> their conscience . . . you sin against Christ (1 Cor.
> 8:12, RSV).

My disillusionment with churches and church members
came in my early years as reporter on a small town newspaper. I knew for a fact that some of the leading churchmen were falsifying their tax returns. One man, prominent
in his church, owned squalid rental property in the "Negro
quarters" on which he boasted of a 20 per cent net return.
The courts and law enforcement officers practiced unconcealed discrimination against "niggers" and "poor
whites," notwithstanding church affiliation on the part of
judges and police.

This was the period of the "muckrakers," a term applied
to a group of authors and journalists whose specialty was
the exposure of corruption in the business and politics of
the United States. Among these were Lincoln Steffens,
Ida Tarbell, George Creel, T. W. Lawson, Ray Stannard
Baker, Mark Sullivan, Samuel Hopkins Adams, and Upton
Sinclair.

Upton Sinclair's *The Jungle,* a sordid novel of the Chicago stockyards, fascinated me.

In a small way, I undertook some "muckraking" feature
articles, which aroused the ire of the local VIPs and

brought me a measure of both favorable and unfavorable notice.

My conversion changed many attitudes, developed new interests and loyalties, but did not rid me of my disappointment that the churches and churchmen apparently had so little concern for social righteousness. Imagine my surprise and delight, then, when I enrolled at Southern Seminary in a Christian sociology class taught by Dr. Charles S. Gardner. Here was a man after my own heart—a transparent and committed Christian, with as sensitive social conscience as a Lincoln Steffens or a Mark Sullivan or an Upton Sinclair.

Dr. Gardner at once introduced the class to Walter Rauschenbusch, who was then at the height of his career as leader of the Christian social movement in America. As pastor of a German Baptist church in Brooklyn, New York, in a field adjacent to Hell's Kitchen, a slum area, Rauschenbusch had come to see that it was not enough to rescue a single soul from sin; his social environment must also be saved.

To him, the bringing in of the kingdom of God on earth demanded the regeneration of society as well as individuals. His *Christianity and the Social Crisis,* interpreted and reinforced by the professor, gave to us a new perspective for our preaching and pastoral ministry. We realized that it would be difficult for us ever again to be complacent concerning social evils and injustices.

Dr. Gardner's election to the seminary faculty was to teach homiletics—the art of preaching. He succeeded Dr. E. C. Dargan, who had retired in 1907 to return to the pastorate. The trustees were faced with the necessity of electing someone to take Dargan's place. President Mullins had no recommendation. As the matter was being discussed, a trustee arose and placed in nomination Charles Spurgeon Gardner, who at the time was pastor of Grace Street Baptist Church, Richmond, Virginia. The word of his preaching power, combined with authentic scholarship, had gone abroad. The nomination was unanimously approved and he entered his notable career as seminary professor, to be terminated at retirement thirty-two years later.

Traditionally, teachers of homiletics had been chiefly concerned with *how* to preach. Dr. Gardner was more concerned with *what* to preach. He realized that the trend of the times was in the direction of social betterment of the people. He was deeply concerned lest secular forces outrun Christian leadership of this tremendously significant movement. He saw socialism and the labor movement growing away from the churches and becoming more and more estranged from Christianity. Communism was beginning to rear its ugly head, threatening the very existence of the Christian religion. To ignore this rising tide of secularism and materialistic atheism would result in preaching losing its relevance. He deplored the use of the term "social gospel," since there is but one gospel— the good news of salvation through Christ for all who repent and believe. But in the growing complexity of life, salvation could no longer be thought of as purely personal. Christian principles must be applied to the human situation or the preacher and his church would lose significance and importance.

The controversy over the "social gospel" put Dr.

Gardner under the spotlight. The seminary had for years been the favorite object of attack by certain right wing or "fundamentalist" preachers. Some of them now un-limbered their guns on Dr. Gardner, assuming that his course in Christian sociology was of necessity in support of the "Social Gospel" heresy. Completely unruffled, Dr. Gardner pursued his even, sweet-tempered way, refusing to make any reply in his defense.

Later, when he was attacked from the Convention plat-form, some of his former students who loved him begged him to reply. "No," he said firmly, "No. In the light of eternity, what difference would it make?"

Others of our seminary professors the students admired, sometimes even feared. But Dr. Gardner they loved. He counted himself simply as "first among equals."

I shall never forget the first occasion when I went to his office. He arose and stood deferentially until I was seated! This was his characteristic attitude of respect for personality. The seminary employed a Negro janitor. "Hill" we all called him, that is, all but Dr. Gardner, who spoke of him and to him as "Mr. Hill." There was nothing forced or ostentatious about this attitude—it was a reflection of his innate disposition. He could be severe in his criticism of the poor sermons handed in by the students, but he was never caustic.

On one occasion he was talking to the class about emo-tion in preaching. He was unsparing in his rejection of emotionalism, the effort to play on the emotions of an audience for effect. Yet, he declared, there was a time when the preacher, deeply moved, was justified in lift-ing his voice and pounding the pulpit for emphasis.

At the next meeting of the class he said, in effect: "I want to retract what I said about emotion expressing itself in loud language and noisy gesture. I was mistaken. When emotion is deep and genuine, it tends toward the lowering of the voice, the tensing of the muscles, and the restraint of gesture." He then gave several examples from literature and from his own experience and observation, and called on the class to confirm his conclusion from their experiences. As we went away from the class, a student remarked, "It takes a big man to say, 'I was mistaken.'"

A deacon told of calling Dr. Gardner and requesting a pulpit supply. A student was selected from the preaching class and sent for the service. The next week a second call came but the deacon requested that another man be sent. Again the call came for a "supply" preacher and again there was the strict stipulation to send another man. When the fourth call came with the same insistence that another man be sent, Dr. Gardner's curiosity was aroused. "What's the matter with the students I've sent you?" he inquired of the deacon. "Couldn't they preach?"

"They could preach all right," responded the deacon, "but they must have been told something dreadful about us. Every one of them has taken as his text the Eighth Commandment, 'Thou shalt not steal.' Who's been talking to the students about us? We don't like it."

Then the truth dawned upon the professor: he had assigned this text for a written sermon to be handed in by the students for criticism and revision. So impressed were they by the way in which the professor had helped them to unfold the subject that each one tried it out on a congregation the first chance he got.

When the Southern Baptist Convention met at Jacksonville, Florida, in 1911, Dr. Gardner was the Convention preacher. Realizing that he was under fire, and shrinking from publicity, he was determined to bring a message that would set him right in the eyes of his brethren and at the same time avoid the controversial. His sermon was titled: "The Coming of the Kingdom."

So deeply concerned were the students that, at the time of the delivery of the sermon, they gathered spontaneously in the prayer room of New York Hall and spent the hour praying for their beloved professor. It has been said that few sermons ever preached before the Convention so greatly moved the audience as did Dr. Gardner's on this occasion. The verdict was overwhelmingly expressed, "He is preaching and teaching the gospel of Jesus Christ."

It was a fortunate circumstance that the teacher of homiletics should have taught also the course in Christian sociology. To the traditional "how" of preaching were added the who and what and why. Preaching thus became far more than the art of preparing and delivering a sermon. Under Dr. Gardner's guidance, the young preacher concentrated his concern on the persons to whom the sermon was preached, the relevance of the sermon's content for the congregation, and the social and ethical implications of the biblical revelation.

Out of a study of general psychology and the psychology of religion came Dr. Gardner's *Psychology and Preaching* (1918). Educational psychology had found a firm place in the study and practice of teaching; he clearly perceived that the newly developing science of human nature and conduct was equally valuable and applicable to preaching.

His writing reflects the psychology of that era, which gathered about the study of instincts, faculties, stimulus and response, the emotions, attention, and suggestion, with growing concern for the "occupational and group mind." While not professing to be a trained psychologist, Dr. Gardner explored the extant literature with great thoroughness and derived from his wide reading many keen insights for the preacher and his preaching. In all of this, he was at least twenty years ahead of his time.

The major thrust of Dr. Gardner's teaching and writing was increasingly in the field of Christian social ethics. The mounting concern for the common man had become a mighty ground swell. He realized that Jesus and his gospel needed to be reinterpreted in terms of his concept of "the kingdom of God . . . on earth," according to which Jesus proposed the regeneration of the whole social order. He did not expect such a transformation to come suddenly, as Dr. Gardner interpreted the mind of Christ, but by a gradual process, with occasional upheavals and catastrophic changes.

Jesus, he said, "projected into the world a great dynamic organizing social principle, or energy, which was to spread and to penetrate through and through the social organism, transforming it from within; so that ultimately all its activities would be performed in a new spirit, and all its forms changed and adapted to express the character of the new life." [1]

He had no illusions about the saving of men en masse,

---

[1] Charles S. Gardner, *The Ethics of Jesus and Social Progress* (New York: George H. Doran Co., 1914), p. 75.

for always at the center of the saved society is the saved person. The saved individual, however, is saved from exploitation, predatory wealth, criminality, ignorance, poverty, and disease. To be saved *from* sin means to be saved *to* self-realization through service, to the abundant life, to responsible and active citizenship, to happiness in the family and the nurture of physically and spiritually healthy children.

Dr. Gardner's optimism concerning the upward climb of man received a rude shock when, in the very year his book was published, World War I erupted. Should we honor him any less because of his hope that "war—and every form of conflict between men—is more and more coming under the prohibition of this conscience; . . . while . . . the passion for humanity is growing stronger as the spirit of the Son of man spreads through the hearts of men and draws them into a universal and ethical brotherhood"? [2]

I once overheard a conversation between two preachers at a convention. One asked, "What has become of Charlie Gardner?" His companion replied, "He has retired into the obscurity of a professorship at Southern Seminary." True, Dr. Gardner was not in the limelight during these years of his pioneering as a teacher and author; but he was quickening the conscience of a whole generation of preachers and pastors to whom he gave a new and dynamic interpretation of the Christian gospel in its ethical and social implications and application.

Dr. Gardner's conscience-quickening teaching did not

---

[2] *Ibid.,* p. 356.

sink as deep into the thought and practice of the churches as he hoped it might. In his retirement years at Richmond, Virginia, he sometimes expressed his keen disappointment that the people whom he loved and to whom he had given a lifetime of teaching were strangely insensitive to the economic and racial issues that were beginning to loom like a dark and threatening cloud on the horizon. Who knows but that the South and the nation might have been spared much of the strife and hurt that have come a generation later if the prophetic voice of Charles Gardner had been heard and heeded?

With clear vision he saw that the new day will not be brought in by a sudden revolution among adults but by winning the oncoming generation to Christ and developing in them an effective Christian consciousness. Never spoke prophet more truly than when Dr. Gardner said: "The Future is always lying at the breast of the Present. . . . There may be other important interests at stake; but however important, they all recede into the background in the presence of this; for in the children the *whole* future is at stake." [3]

Well may we who still believe in the kingdom of God, both as a present and a future reality, listen to this great teacher whose stirring of our conscience may yet make the difference between a righteous social order and world disaster.

---

[3] *Ibid.*, pp. 320–21.

6

Isaac Jacobus Van Ness

Editor-Teacher

Write what you see . . . and send it to the . . .
churches (Rev. 1:11, RSV).

The formal teaching experience of Isaac Jacobus Van
Ness, so far as I know, was confined to a Sunday school
class. Yet as I think of my teachers, I am bound to put him
in the select list. For thirty-five years, first as general editor
and then as executive secretary-treasurer of the Baptist
Sunday School Board of the Southern Baptist Convention,
he did much to direct the thinking and cement the unity
of a great and growing body of churches. He brought to
his task the unique equipment of one born and reared
outside the ranks of the people whom he served, yet deeply
committed to their principles and purposes. Thus his heritage gave to him a breadth of understanding that a born
and bred Southern Baptist might not have had.

Should the writer-editor be included in the category of
teachers? When we think of a teacher, we usually have
in mind someone in face-to-face dialogue with a group
of learners. May we concede that one is also a teacher who
addresses his learners through a manuscript that has been
committed to the printed page?

Certainly the Bible would justify the inclusion of writers
in the category of teachers. What would have become of
the teachings of Moses and the prophets if what they

taught had not been written and thus preserved for future generations? What would have been the consequences if the four evangelists and the New Testament interpreters had not written concerning the life and teachings of Jesus Christ? How would teachers teach if they did not have content for their teaching provided in books?

I. J. Van Ness conceived his ministry as a ministry of writing. Harold Englund might well have been thinking of Dr. Van Ness when he wrote:

> The Christian writer is a teacher, an analyst, a prophet, a comforter, an angry conscience. He needs to be caught up into the presence of God and remain there until something of a divine perspective anoints his spirit and suffuses his work. . . . Unless the hand of God is resting upon the shoulder of the Christian writer, however, his work is vanity. But with this divine accreditation, the Christian writer will be able to transfer the power and the glory from his own vital relationship with God to the printed page. . . .
>
> Writing is a ministry. It is a ministry symbolized by a desk piled high with work in process . . . by deadlines, letters to the editor, the anxiety of late manuscripts, reject notices. If a pulpit is an instrument of ministering, so is a sheet of white paper, poised in a typewriter, waiting for the costly fruit of mental toil and prayerful concern to be yielded up in loving obedience to him who is Lord of all.[1]

It was with something of this spirit of dedication that Dr. Van Ness devoted half a lifetime to the writing, editing, publishing, and promotion of the literature that poured in increasing volume from the presses of the Baptist Sunday School Board.

---

[1] "Writing Is a Ministry," *Christianity Today,* VI (September 28, 1962), 4–6.

The Van Ness ancestors settled in New Jersey, where
Isaac Jacobus was born July 15, 1860. His father was
caretaker of the estate of the elder Samuel Colgate of
Orange, New Jersey, whose son Russell Colgate was for
many years prominent in Sunday school circles. At seven-
teen Isaac was converted under the preaching of Dr.
Edward Judson, son of the noted missionary. Young Isaac
was made secretary of the Sunday school of which Mr.
Colgate was superintendent.

On finishing high school, the young man became book-
keeper for J. P. Morgan and Company, New York City.
One morning, as he sat on his high stool at the long desk,
he paused and looked contemplatively at the line of fellow
bookkeepers—many of them stooped and gray from long
years of service. "Surely there is something better in life
for me than this!" he said to himself. Acting on the impulse,
he went to the office and resigned.

Being interested in religious work, young Van Ness ob-
tained employment in the New York YMCA. Among other
duties, he served as athletic director. His interest in religious activities steadily grew. One day Dr. J. T. Dickin-
son, his pastor, asked him what good reason he had for
not preaching. The idea took root and developed into the
conviction that he was called to the Christian ministry.
Talking the matter over with Mr. Colgate, he was advised
to attend a southern seminary, since, according to Mr.
Colgate, southern preachers were more warmhearted and
more effective than those in the North. A comparative
study of seminary catalogs and an opportunity to hear
Dr. John A. Broadus preach led to the decision to enrol
in the seminary at Louisville.

Dr. Van Ness never tired of paying tribute to Dr. Broadus and of telling of his influence on his life. One of his choice stories was that on an occasion Dr. Broadus sent him to the blackboard to write the outline of a sermon. The outline was developed in minute detail and covered the whole board. Dr. Broadus surveyed it critically, then remarked, "A very good skeleton, a *very* good skeleton—but not enough meat!"

Another favorite story was of the brash student who kept interrupting Dr. Broadus. The great teacher summoned the student to the desk, handed him the Bible and roll book, and commanded him to take over. The student stammered for a few minutes, then stood speechless. Dr. Broadus cupped his hands together and began to blow, expanding his hands as if inflating a balloon. With a swift jab of his forefinger he punctured the balloon and hissed while it collapsed. Dr. Van Ness delighted to tell this story when he wanted slyly to apply it to one who thought more highly of himself than he ought to think.

While at Louisville, Dr. Van Ness fell in love with Frances Tabb, daughter of a socially prominent family. The Tabbs had higher ambitions for their talented daughter than marriage to a struggling young Baptist preacher. But Frances saw in this young man what others may not have seen and in 1891 they were married. In later years she happily testified that hers had been a far richer and fuller life than that of her girl friends who had married men of greater wealth and professional prominence.

Upon graduating from the seminary, Dr. Van Ness was called as pastor of Immanuel Baptist Church, Nashville. During his pastorate of six years he became intimately acquainted with Dr. J. M. Frost, who gave to him occasional writing assignments. His writing ability called him to the attention of Dr. T. P. Bell, editor of the Georgia *Christian Index*. Thus he became associate in the editorship of this leading Southern Baptist newspaper. In 1900 he was elected editorial secretary of the Sunday School Board and returned to Nashville for his great lifework.

My acquaintance with Dr. Van Ness began in 1916. Two years before graduating from Southern Seminary, I was serving a pastorate in New Albany, Mississippi. In the autumn of 1916 a telegram came from Dr. Van Ness, requesting that I come to Nashville for an interview. The end was clearly approaching for Dr. Frost and he and Dr. Van Ness were looking for an editorial assistant.

I had grown up in a newspaper office, had earned my journeyman printer's union card, and had written my doctoral thesis on Southern Baptist religious journalism. Dr. Van Ness pointed to a pile of letters on his desk and explained that they were recommendations of men for the associate editorship. Somehow, he said, my name kept turning up on top and he had taken that as a providential sign that I should be invited to consider the job. He took me to see Dr. Frost, who was on his deathbed. I shall never forget the pale, wan figure that lay on the bed nor the clasp of the thin hands as Dr. Frost joined in the invitation to me to become Dr. Van Ness's helper. His last words were, "Young man, a great and effectual door is being opened to you."

Dr. Frost died before I reached Nashville. Dr. Van Ness was elected to succeed him as executive secretary. He continued to give considerable time to the editorial work, but more and more of it fell on me and on Miss Marian Phelps, a capable Presbyterian woman who assisted with manuscript editing and preparation of copy for the printers. Gradually the responsibilities of the secretary's office absorbed Dr. Van Ness's time and energy, so that for awhile the burden of the editorial duties was largely on my shoulders. My special assignment was the missionary magazine, *Home and Foreign Fields,* which the Convention had requested the Board to publish. Dr. Van Ness was proud of the magazine and of the Sunday School Board's vigorous promotion of home and foreign missions.

I am indebted to the late John L. Hill for a story that throws much light on the Christian character of Dr. Van Ness:

One of the greatest pastors in Nashville had a weakness for beverage alcohol and occasionally would yield to the temptation. He was a member of the Sunday School Board and a personal friend of Dr. Van Ness. One year they went to the Convention together and shared a hotel room in the Convention city. One day, as Dr. Van Ness strolled through the halls of the Convention building, he missed his friend. At once he thought he had better look him up. He returned to the hotel, opened their room door with his own key and walked in. There sat his friend by the desk with a bottle of whiskey before him. The government stamp had been torn off, and the stopper had been moved up and down, but no liquor had gone from the flask. Dr. Van Ness said, "Well, I think we have had enough of the Convention, let's go home." And the executive secretary of the Sunday School Board, whose presence presumably was required at the Convention, left the Convention to take his friend out of temptation. I loved him immediately upon hearing this story, and my love for him deepened through the years. He was a great Christian.

By 1900, the Sunday school increasingly was becoming a powerful agency of the churches. In England, where it originated, the Sunday school continued to be largely a children's affair. In the United States, its enrolment had been enlarged to include young people and adults. The Baraca-Philathea Organized Class Movement greatly increased its influence and prestige. The Sunday school was a lay institution, largely dependent on untrained men and women as officers and teachers.

Dr. Van Ness was quick to perceive the strategic advantage of the Sunday school for Baptist churches. He also realized that the Sunday school must be made educationally respectable if it was to fulfil its mission.

Certain requirements were, therefore, obvious: the literature for officers, teachers, and pupils must be of high quality; there must be a simple, workable plan of officer-teacher training; the Sunday school must be the teaching agency of the church, not a separate institution; the high purposes of the Sunday school and effective methods of teaching and administration must be taken directly to the churches through co-operation with the several states of the Convention; the Baptist Young People's Union (later the Baptist Training Union) must be expanded to include all ages and made the training agency of the churches; all the work of the Board must be shot through and through with the spirit of evangelism and missions. To the achievement of these ends, Dr. Van Ness gave himself with unflagging zeal throughout his long and remarkable career.

Dr. Van Ness saw with unerring judgment that the success of the Sunday school and the Training Union goes

back to the pastor, the general officers, the leaders and
teachers, and the individual members of classes and un-
ions. In those early days, we faced a colossal task—to provide Bible study and membership training materials of
high quality that would yet be inexpensive; to make the
helps sound educationally and yet within the reach of
many officers and teachers with meager education; to keep
the literature true to the fundamentals of the Baptist
faith, yet in line with progressive biblical scholarship; to
provide training for officers and teachers and leaders on
the level where they were, yet with a plan that would
challenge them to continuous improvement; to accept
the distinctiveness of the Baptist mission and message,
yet maintain a spirit of cordial fellowship toward other
evangelical Christians; to make the Sunday school and
Training Union means toward evangelism, missions, and
stewardship, yet always within the framework of Bible
study; to provide bookstore outlets that would encourage
church members to read more widely; and to do all this
with financing so soundly based that the Board could op-
erate at a profit and thus be an asset to all other denominational enterprises without calling on the churches for
aid.

Dr. Van Ness was no superman, as he would have cheer-
fully admitted. His genius lay more in his ability to gather
about him dedicated men and women who could do the
job. As they learned from him, he learned from them.
Southern Baptists can never repay the debt of gratitude
they owe to these devoted men and women who formed
the staff of which Dr. Van Ness was chief: Harvey Beau-
champ, Prince E. Burroughs, Edwin C. Dargan, Arthur

Flake, Landrum Leavell, John L. Hill, Hight C Moore, E. E. Lee, William P. Phillips, B. W. Spilman, Harry Strickland, W. S. Wiley, Miss Lillian Forbes, Miss Annie Williams, and others of the gallant pioneers whose creative and sacrificial labors laid the foundations of the tremendous institution which the Sunday School Board has come to be.

The Ecumenical or "Union" Movement was looming on the horizon during the editorial and administrative ministries of Dr. Van Ness. He did much to guide Southern Baptists to take a sensible, middle course in their attitude toward Christian unity. With keen insight he perceived two contrasting difficulties—that of isolationism on the one hand and loss of identity on the other.

A case in point was the type of lessons to be used. A grave difficulty was confronted. The International Uniform Lesson System had done much to popularize and unify the Sunday schools of North America. A Baptist layman, B. F. Jacobs, was a leader in the inauguration of the system. Dr. John A. Broadus was among the first chairmen of the lessons committee and was succeeded by Dr. John R. Sampey. The committee was interdenominational, which made its work suspect to some groups in the Convention. Without hesitation Dr. Van Ness threw all the weight of his position and influence in favor of co-operation with the committee and the International Association and later with the reorganized International Council of Religious Education.

While yielding nothing of the essentials of his denomination's position and convictions, he thus kept Southern Baptists in the great stream of national and worldwide

Sunday school work. Not only did this bring signal benefits to Southern Baptist churches, it also contributed much to the strength of the growing Sunday school movement, nationally and internationally.

From that early day, a vast and increasing stream of printed helps for Bible study and membership-leadership training has poured from the Sunday School Board to give stimulation and guidance to multiplying millions of the people called Baptists. Others have entered into his labors, but Dr. Van Ness stood at a turning point and gave direction to the amazing future of his people. Through his writing ministry he made a difference! By this test he deserves a place in the list of great teachers of his generation. Dr. Van Ness spoke as teacher, whose teaching continues even now to provide guidelines, when he wrote:

We must always maintain toward others the attitude of respect. It is no compliment to our own belief to sneer at the belief of another man; to sneer at our brother's convictions is to lead somebody to sneer at our convictions. If we believe truth to be sacred, and, therefore, to be sacredly obeyed, we must have the same respect for every other man in the world who is trying to live up to that which he believes. No spirit is more destructive than the spirit of censorious or belittling criticism. Even when we cannot comprehend how certain beliefs can hold sway over the hearts of men, we must needs respect those who hold these convictions. There may be times when we suspect selfishness and self-interest as impelling some of the teachers of truth. We must be slow to believe this, and when we do believe it we shall have to turn away in a spirit of sorrow. Even then we must not have the spirit of lightness and levity. Ridicule is a poor weapon in religious warfare. This respectful attitude to others grows out of our doctrine of soul-liberty and our principle of personal and spiritual religion, and not from indifference toward the welfare of truth.[2]

When we bear in mind that these words were written in 1914, and that this text has been in the list of study course books for two generations, we may well appreciate how it influenced "the Baptist spirit" toward a sound and constructive view of relationships with other Christian bodies.

If the measure of the teacher is that *he made a difference,* Isaac Jacobus Van Ness assuredly belongs in the list. By his life, by his pen, by his guidance of other writers and teachers, by his wise direction of an educational publishing institution, by his leadership of the teaching and training program of an expanding education-conscious denomination, he inaugurated and influenced changes that have continued past his lifetime into the present, and will continue into the distant future.

Because of this quiet, modest, far-seeing man, the Bible is better known and loved throughout the Baptist world—and beyond. There need be no hesitation in assigning Dr. Van Ness a high place in the list of great teachers of his generation. Unquestionably, *he made a difference.*

---

[2] *Training in the Baptist Spirit* (Nashville: Sunday School Board, SBC, 1914), pp. 87–88.

7
George Albert Coe
Educational Revolutionary

Of how much more value is a man than a sheep
(Matt. 12:12, RSV).

My first four years on the faculty of Southern Seminary
were both challenging and disillusioning. I found myself
in the midst of masters in their fields—Old Testament
and Hebrew, New Testament and Greek, theology and
philosophy, church history and apologetics, homiletics
and social ethics. To me, the newcomer, was assigned the
course in "Sunday school pedagogy," which had first grown
out of a series of annual lectures on the Sunday school.
This emphasis had been developed into a brief course
taught by Dr. Byron H. DeMent, who became president
of New Orleans Baptist Seminary; and then by Dr. Landrum Leavell, loaned to Southern Seminary by the Sunday
School Board for a semester of the session. The traditional course in practical theology had been renamed
"church efficiency," since Dr. Mullins did not like the word
"practical" applied to "theology," as if implying that his
courses in theology were not practical!

Throughout the world of theological education there
were stirrings of discontent because the curriculum was
too content-centered and inadequately oriented toward
equipping the student for effectiveness in pastoral ministries. Inevitable tensions developed between those who

taught the traditional theological disciplines and those who were undertaking to bring to the curriculum the newer so-called "practical" courses.

While I was cordially received into the fellowship of the faculty as a person, I perceived that what I was assigned to teach lacked academic respectability. I soon discovered that the students shared this view. I learned that my friend and fellow student, John M. Price, who had previously been called to Southwestern Seminary for the same type of service, was experiencing like difficulty. Investigation disclosed that similar tensions had developed at other theological institutions—Union Seminary of New York, Yale Divinity School, University of Chicago Divinity School, Princeton, Vanderbilt, and others.

Summer courses in education convinced me that something radical would be necessary if "Sunday school pedagogy" was to be replaced by courses with reputable standing in religious education. I saw clearly that there were not two sets of principles in education—secular principles, applicable to the teaching of public school subjects on the one hand and "spiritual" principles, applicable to the teaching of the Bible and religious subjects on the other.

Casting about for an answer, I discovered the work of George Albert Coe, then professor of religious education in Teachers College, Columbia University. Here was a man of first-rate ability, teaching in the foremost teachers' college of America, who was giving my field the standing which I knew it deserved. The trustees approved my application for a leave of absence and I headed for New York City to put my hunch to the test.

When my application for graduate study had been processed and approved, I requested Dr. Coe as faculty adviser. I sat in his room patiently waiting until finally he looked up from a pile of papers on his desk and came over and sat down beside me. He was not exceptionally impressive in appearance but friendly and keenly alert. He looked over my credentials, asked me a few questions, then turned to the catalog and schedule card to help me work out my study program.

"I want you to have something with John Dewey," he said, "this may be his last year of teaching on the Hill, since he is planning to retire." Then, he continued, "I want you to have something with Thorndike . . . and Kilpatrick . . . and McMurray . . . and Harrison Elliott over at Union Seminary . . . and—"

"Wait a minute," I interrupted. "What are these men teaching?"

"I don't care *what* they are teaching," he retorted. "You probably know more now than you are able to teach. I want you to expose yourself to some master teachers, to observe their methods and objectives, to study their personality and philosophy—not to imitate them but to find yourself and determine the course you will pursue in a lifetime of teaching." I took his advice and a new world opened up to me as I studied not only books and subject matter but great teachers in action.

The winds of change blew on me from many directions. Residence in New York City was in itself a life-changing experience. John Dewey was an upsetting educational radical, with his philosophy of instrumentalism and his insistence that the school should be society in miniature, where learning is experience leading to more enriched experience, and where teaching is stimulation and guidance of experience in preparation of the learner to do better what he is going to have to do anyhow.

Thorndike, with massive frame and head and massive intellect to match, led us through labyrinths of educational psychology to a better understanding of the teaching-learning processes and to an understanding of levels of intelligence and individual differences.

William Heard Kilpatrick, the most popular teacher of the group, brought educational philosophy down to earth and fascinated us with his interpretation of philosophy in terms of schoolroom practice. Harrison Sackett Elliott was almost obsessed with his concept of teaching through the discussion method, in which he insisted that teaching is stimulation to discussion and learning is participation in group thinking.

The central figure among these and other teachers at Columbia University and Union Seminary was for me George Albert Coe. I was in a seminar in which he led us to confront the question, "What is Christian education?" Years later, Dr. Coe wrote his last and perhaps most effective book under this title. He did not quiz us on textbook materials nor stand before us to lecture. He identified himself with us, became one of us, was an inquiring student alongside us, took his share of assignments, and somehow made us feel that we were as important as he.

Dr. Coe's viewpoints we absorbed rather than received by transmission. His *Social Theory of Religious Education* had just appeared and was used as reference. The thesis of his book is that religious (Christian) education must seek to help men live as Christians in a righteous social order, not just to know what the Bible says and what Christian doctrines teach. The purpose of religious education, Dr. Coe insisted, is to bring growing persons into an ever-increasing awareness of God in Christ as controlling the whole of life in all areas of human living. We are, therefore, not to teach *lessons,* but *persons.*

Educational principles and processes in the field of religion are no different from those in any other field, he contended. Education becomes Christian when its objectives are those of Jesus Christ—the "democracy of God" on earth. He said that "if the Gospels were being written today the writers would probably use the word 'democracy' instead of 'kingdom,' since Christianity demands the ultimate overthrow of all earthly kingships and the establishment of equality and justice among men." To the objection that this emphasis neglected the redemptive purpose of Christianity, Dr. Coe replied by inquiring as to what was included in salvation—"the soul" or the total personality in a saved society?

Dr. Coe challenged strongly the transmissive theory of teaching. He sought to show that "teaching the Bible" as transmitting from teacher to pupil biblical facts, ideas, doctrines, and ideals gave no assurance of carry-over into conduct and character. Over against this "transmissive" method of teaching he put what he called "the creative." By this he meant the reaction of learner to teacher and to materials of teaching, so that changes actually occur not only in persons but in social conditions.

He pointed out that the transmissive method, a chief dependence of teachers through the centuries, had not only failed to bring about vital Christianization but actually had resulted all too often in preserving the status quo. He opened our eyes to see that the chief bulwark of despotism in church and state through the centuries had been authoritarian transmission of the tradition. "When people discover truth for themselves," he said, "they will revolt against error and wrong."

"Give children all the facts," he was fond of saying, "and nine times out of ten they will judge wisely and justly. Purposeful activity on the part of the pupil," he insisted, "is the most educative experience in the world." He was not a special advocate of the "project method," but he saw in its wise use a means of involving teacher and learners in creative educational experiences that would develop effective moral responsibility.

Dr. Coe felt strongly that his "creative experience" view of religious education would not mean less but more use of the Bible and biblical literature. The genius of the biblical revelation is to be found in this principle of interaction, as God dealt with men and men responded to him. According to this view, the Bible was not given just that men might know what God said but that their reaction to him might make them more Godlike persons.

God, he held, delights in honest inquiry and continues to make himself and his truth known through those who ask, seek, and knock. Dr. Coe saw no objection to the application of scientific principles of investigation to religious problems but rather insisted that the scientific method was far superior to the old logical deduction used to establish and maintain dogmatism. He erased the boundary between "secular" and "religious" learning, and never ceased to express regret that ministers and Sunday school teachers seemed to ascribe some sort of magical power to the Scriptures that made its teaching and learning different from the teaching and learning of other subjects.

He believed that the best possible methods should be used in the teaching of the Bible and religious truth. These best methods would make them no less Christian.

Dr. Coe had little patience with anything that smacked of the "magical." Yet he was always reverent in his attitude toward God, Jesus Christ, the Bible, the church, the Christian religion. He held that superstition was the foe of real religion and that true science was its great friend.

Once when a student asked him somewhat cautiously, "Are you not a radical?" Dr. Coe replied, "Yes, indeed I am—I like to go to the root of things, as the word implies."

Dr. Coe had retired from the faculty of Union Seminary and had moved across the street to teach in the University as emeritus. He no longer was as militant as once he had been. The years had softened him and brought him back to a greater emphasis on personal religion.

One cold winter night he met with a group of students at an informal tea in which he stated his subject as, "Why I am no Longer a Liberal." He hastened to say that this by no means meant that he had become a "Fundamentalist" but that a review of the results of his teaching, especially of graduate students, had led him to see that he had overemphasized the scientific approach and method in education and had not made enough place for a personal God revealed in Jesus Christ.

He related that he had had three conversion experiences: first, as a lad in an old-fashioned Methodist revival; second, to his scientific-social concept of religious education; third, to a deepened faith in the redemptive power of God in Christ and of lessened faith in science. The last had come in light of the relative failure of the scientific method to save the world from the terrible disasters which war and crime had brought. The conversation that night was intimate and personal, not intended for public report, but it revealed the spiritual depth and intellectual honesty of a great teacher.

I count George Albert Coe one of my great teachers because he made a difference. I have found myself going back again and again to his statement of objective in religious education: "Growth of the young toward, and into, mature and efficient devotion to the democracy of God and a happy self-realization therein." The expansion of this statement into its particulars and then their implementation have formed the framework of the creative teaching in the field of religion which has characterized the best in the new era of church school education.

His was the formative influence that did much to give direction and vitality to the concepts and processes which have led teaching and training in the churches, as well as in seminaries and Christian schools, to academic acceptability and spiritual fruitfulness.

When Dr. Coe died in 1951, in his eighty-ninth year, a memorial edition of *Religious Education* (official publication of the Religious Education Association) was devoted to an evaluation and appreciation of his long and useful life. The president of the Association, Samuel P. Franklin, wrote:

George Albert Coe was the outstanding religious educator of the first half of the twentieth century. His long and active life and his creative thought are inextricably interwoven with those years. He met the problems of his days in such a spirit and with such resources that the patterns of thought which he molded are still being used in a vital manner and bid fair to be used for years to come.

His long life as teacher, writer, and crusader for the cause of liberal thought and aggressive action in education and religion has inspired his contemporaries, while blazing a trail for leaders of future generations.[1]

His contemporary in the Divinity School of the University of Chicago, Ernest Chave, wrote:

Did Coe make a significant contribution to religious education? Can any individual hope to make any important difference in the philosophy, methods, or practices of religious education? Coe believed that the growth process was the most outstanding characteristic of man and his world. He believed that man could increasingly come to an understanding of this growth process in the areas of moral and religious living, and that man had a responsibility to exercise a creative force in development of meanings, values, and progressive achievements. He did not shut his eyes to difficult facts but he believed from his observations and studies that mankind was learning, and that the developments in education were enabling man to gain insights, clarify objectives, and to make specific advances in moral and religious living. He spent his life in trying to understand this forward movement and to share in its varied activities.[2]

To teachers and students of the succeeding generation, Dr. Coe's significance was well stated by Frank W. Herri-

---

[1] XLVII (March–April, 1952), 66.
[2] *Ibid.*, 71.

ott, as quoted by Arthur L. Swift, Jr., of Union Theological
Seminary:

> Central in his philosophy and practices were two comple-
> mentary commitments: a scientific attitude toward all facts,
> and a loving attitude toward all persons. Out of these sprang
> his passion for social justice and his conviction that the social
> issues of the present are "the call of God to our pupils." [3]

The years since 1920 have witnessed many advances
in religious education, but perhaps none has been more
significant than the lifting of the ministry of religious education to a recognized and respected vocational level.
The "paid superintendent" of the Sunday school gave
way to the competent "educational director," who in turn
has been superseded by the "minister of education." In
theological seminary circles the movement has been from
occasional lectures and conferences on Sunday school
work to tolerated courses on Sunday school methods to
religious education in the curriculum on a parity with
the old-line classical disciplines. Small churches have
grown larger and large churches have grown to greatness
because of the centrality of religious education in their
organization and activities.

Whether it is fully realized or not, George Albert
Coe is due much credit for these transformations. He
labored and others have entered into his labor and its
fruits—some unawares, others with keen awareness and
appreciation. Through his long lifetime of teaching and
writing, *he made a difference,* and by this measure must
be accounted a place in the list of great teachers.

---

[3] *Ibid.,* 95.

8
Gaines S. Dobbins

Motivator
of Individual Initiative

WAYNE E. OATES [1]

I had not met Dr. Dobbins before I came to the campus of the Southern Baptist Theological Seminary in 1943. Yet, upon enrolling for my first classes, I felt that if there was anything I needed to know worse than how to administer a church, I could not visualize what it would be. I had worked in many churches and knew that they were badly in need of what Dr. Dobbins called pastoral leadership. Therefore, I took church administration and an elective called "psychology of religion" under Dr. Dobbins.

My introduction to Dr. Dobbins, then, was in his classroom. I was impressed with the fact that he had already prepared his lecture material in his workbook. This had been mimeographed and served as the basis for class participation. We called this book "Dobbinology." He had a knack for picking up the humor of students; therefore, he himself referred to it this way, too.

He expected students to read, but he did not use "pop" quizzes, memorization and recitation, or prestudied ex-

---

[1] See "A Note from the Publisher" on page 8.

amination questions as techniques of motivating the student to read. This man could teach without such gimmicks. He taught on the philosophy of problem-solving, involvement of students in projects, exploring uncharted areas of learning, and sending the student into the community to find out things from life itself. He held us strictly accountable for the end results of our own efforts to define our purpose and plan in the world as pastors, teachers, evangelists, missionaries, and chaplains.

This is why I have chosen to name him a "motivator of individual initiative." This is what he brought to pass, not only with me, but with many other students whom I could name. He probed deeply into our motivations for learning, enabling us to realize our own genuine selfhood in the process. As Dr. Dobbins says of George Albert Coe, he (Dr. Dobbins) "identified himself with us, became one of us, was an inquiring student alongside us, took his share of the assignments, and somehow made us feel that we were as important as he." The end result was that we were enabled to become our own true selves under God. He resisted mimicry and imitation of himself and demanded of us originality. Thus he *made a difference* by requiring us to be the best self we had to offer.

Teaching as the Investment and Development of Personal Confidence

In the previous pages Dr. Dobbins speaks of his own mother as a teacher: "Mother took for granted that I could do anything that the other children could do and made me believe it. Her insight and confidence in me made a lifelong difference." This Dr. Dobbins did for me. He assumed that I could do anything that any student could, that I *wanted* to learn and grow. He enabled me to believe this myself. He worked at the basal motivation of trust-formation in the student. He assumed that his students were there to learn, until as individual members they proved otherwise. He did not move on the assumption that we would not do the work unless he made us move like quarry slaves with external anxiety-provoking procedures of prodding nature.

I moved into graduate work with Dr. Dobbins as my supervisor. His investment of confidence motivated me to work like fury to master new areas of study that had not been investigated. Dr. Dobbins believed in me when I had real doubts about myself. We explored the relationship between religion and medicine, psychotherapy and the Christian faith, and a Christian apologetic in the fact of the clinical discoveries of psychoanalysis. This was uncharted territory. I wanted to find teachers who had worked all these things out and had the answers. Dr. Dobbins rightly told me that there were none. We would have to work it out on our own. He pledged to sweat it out with me. He never left me as a senior explorer and provocator, nor did he lift his finger to do my thinking for me. But when I wrote something down or discovered new materials, he probed me persistently for the right interpretation and conclusions to the data.

There are real hazards to this investment of confidence. The student does not learn his own limits soon enough. He is likely to take on more responsibility than a person of his age and experience should. This in itself can develop his role as a leader and a teacher before he has had the kind of protection he needs from too much responsibility in order to function most effectively. For example, I found myself taking on much too much responsibility in the early years of my teaching as a junior colleague of Dr. Dobbins. I discharged my tasks fairly well, but I could have done so more effectively if I had more gradually assumed some of these responsibilities.

Overloading students with responsibility must be assessed, however. Dr. Dobbins and the whole faculty worked in an era of depression and wartime economy. There were no funds for increasing the size of the faculty. When a man died, retired, or went to another position, young, inexperienced, and green recruits had to be used. We were known as the "scrub faculty." This name came from football, the "scrub team" being one that was used to scrimmage with the varsity and to pinch-hit in the event of emergency.

In postwar theological education, Southern Baptists have continued a depression-economy attitude toward the support of theological professors. We have had a constant drain of older, more experienced professors into administrative positions in the denomination and out of the classroom. The depression and wartime economy has prevailed in an era of affluence.

Dr. Dobbins set the example of a dedicated teacher whose whole life was given to the classroom. He never allowed his many administrative responsibilities to obscure his dedication to the classroom. He carried very heavy administrative responsibilities throughout Dr. Sampey's administration as president. Dr. Sampey and the trustees had turned to Dr. Dobbins to be the seminary's financial agent (the treasurer without pay). At first the seminary could not even pay the interest on a million-dollar debt, left by Dr. Mullins who died in 1928. Dr. Dobbins spent untold hours effecting economies, meeting with bank officials, negotiating refinancing with an insurance company, finding money in various ways, helping students keep food supplies, saving the downtown property as well as the seminary's credit, and never missing a payroll! All this he did so quietly that very few knew about it, for he was determined not to let administrative responsibility interfere with teaching.

The seminary paid every dime of the debt, endowment was significantly increased, and invested funds emerged worth more than was paid for them. This was the work of many, but the responsibility was squarely on Dr. Dobbins' shoulders.

Teaching as the Direction of the Need to Rebel

I came to the seminary with a chip on my shoulder. I felt that much of the teaching was antiquated, the classes too large, and the "fellow" system of handling students' papers an avoidance of professorial responsibilities. This was true, but my attitude was one of impatience, arrogance, and hardfisted rebellion. However, I worked hard to keep my grades at the top in order to maintain the respect of the persons teaching in a system that tried my patience.

I can recall preaching a sermon in homiletics in which I scored theological education among Southern Baptists for not comparing favorably with the Standard of Excellence for Sunday schools! Often I would use my spare time reading journal articles related to class discussions. For pure mischief, I would ask the professor what he thought of the material in the article. More often than not he had not read the article. Dr. Dobbins was the one exception. I loved to try to catch him off guard. He would listen patiently and say, "I see you are thinking!"

Dr. Dobbins had a way of taking hold of such rebellions and putting them to work. He saw a whole new educational methodology in clinical pastoral education. He saw in this both a challenge to the old presuppositions of theological education and an effective channel into which to direct the rebelliousness of a considerable number of us on the campus at that time. He asked us to put our lives where our mouths were.

He organized a group of students in his psychology of religion class who would give free time as psychiatric aides at Louisville General Hospital in return for an occasional hour of instruction from Dr. Spafford Ackerly, Dr. E. E. Landis, and others associated with them at the University of Louisville Medical School. It was not long before he had us in the harness of a challenging load of tremendous responsibility. I became the group leader of this team of students in my senior year.

Dr. Dobbins gave me what I know now to be an amazing quantity of personal attention for a man as busy as he was. During one of these conferences in his office I began to feel genuinely sorry for having given him such a hard time during my first year. I asked him to forgive me. I told him that if a student did me that way, I feared I could not have been as patient as he had been. He in turn chuckled and said that I should not worry. He said, "If a young mule does not kick the slats out of the barn here the first year, he will be a hopeless conformist by the time he is forty."

Dr. Dobbins understood me and accepted me. He received my rebelliousness with humor and gave it direction toward a target of human suffering that revealed to me my purpose in life. As such a teacher, he made a difference in my life. Through his creative discipline, I was able to discover my true lifework. He turned my rebellion into constructive individuality.

Teaching as Involvement and Participation of Students

One could learn much by listening to Dr. Dobbins and watching him in action. He captured and held attention by reference to field experience with individuals and churches with whom he was working at any given time. He functioned as a consultant to churches and institutions of all kinds and channeled the results of his empirical studies of these situations into the life of his classes. He often referred to himself as a "doctor of sick churches." He was an encourager of well ones, also.

But Dr. Dobbins did not focus attention upon himself. He did not perceive himself as the center of the learning process. He saw himself as the catalyst of learning but not the fountain of knowledge. He tapped other sources of instruction in addition to his own, the most important of which was the interaction of students with each other. Before the National Training Laboratories bequeathed to us the term "buzz" group, Dr. Dobbins would encourage students to talk with each other during the class. If they were mumbling in their beards, he would tactfully encourage them to contribute their reservations about what was being said to the rest of the class. He did this honestly and sincerely, not as a gimmick to get people to quit nudging and talking with each other.

The "project" group was another procedure. He would assign groups of us to work with a given pastor in a local church in order to become really acquainted with what was happening in a real life-situation church. He would use the group solidarity to prod the "gold-bricker" who was loafing on the job. The art of group discipline was the means of involving students in the teaching as well as the learning process.

The group which went to General Hospital as psychiatric aides became a continuing group from year to year. In the third year a specific course content was defined and installed into the curriculum as an elective course. This became the kernel of what is now the basic required course in the pastoral care curriculum of the Southern Baptist Theological Seminary. Other courses were devised that have become clinical pastoral education at Louisville General Hospital and also at Central State Hospital. Similarly, Dr. Dobbins organized a group of women students to take educational oversight of the children of students on the campus. This has evolved into a full-fledged nursery-kindergarten program and is a vital part of the seminary's religious education curriculum.

At the heart of Dr. Dobbins' teaching was the principle of student involvement and participation. This seemed to be cast against the background of the influence of Harrison S. Elliott in his group methodology as well as the problem-solving emphasis of John Dewey and E. L. Thorndike.

But Dr. Dobbins brought to this his own genius. He had compassion for distressed people who needed the working pastor and Christian education director. He focused the attention of enterprising students on the needs of mental patients, little children, working churches. These hot points of concern were the points at which the learning of the student was kindled.

Thus, the student learned in such a way that he could not forget, nor did he have to sweat his heart out in anxiety, wondering whether he was going to be able to remember what the professor wanted. The student knew what the professor wanted and addressed himself to it. Teaching was no life-and-death struggle between teacher and student to see how well they could outwit each other. Teaching and learning comprised a co-operative endeavor between teacher and student, student and student, and student and sufferer in a fellowship of learning.

Teaching as Organizing and Constructing New Forms of Learning Situations

Already it has become apparent that Dr. Dobbins' capacity as an organizer permeated his teaching. He was always organizing and constructing new forms of learning situations. He was a real campaigner in curriculum development. He stood for diversity of teaching methods, broad elective tailoring of the curriculum to meet the individual student's life situation. He was for relevance of the classical in interaction with the contemporary. I never heard him speak disparagingly of the classical subjects of Bible, history, and theology. Rather, he would insist that I "square and plumb" my study of contemporary psychotherapy with the challenge that this brought to my own understanding of these subjects. He resisted the "cream-and-whey" approach of setting the practical over against the classical and the conceptual over against the operational. Yet he stoutly resisted educational imperialism on the basis of the authority of subject matter. Consequently, Dr. Dobbins has made a wide contribution toward diversification of the seminary curriculum. His organizing genius serves him well.

Dr. Dobbins organized the present Department of Psychology of Religion and Pastoral Care. He started this work. He equipped me to carry it to fruition and modestly gave me the credit as a pioneer. But if it had not been for his sponsorship of me and his leadership in the organization of the work, I would never have made it. He was strongly supported in this by J. B. Weatherspoon, Harold Tribble, and Ellis Fuller. Likewise, these four men were the architects of the present Department of Christian Ethics. There Dr. Weatherspoon led the way, and Dr. O. T. Binkley was brought to the seminary to actualize the whole program as a separate department. Dr. Dobbins aided and supported this interaction of Christian ethics with social issues of the day. Likewise, later, Dr. Dobbins continued his pioneer organizing at the curriculum level in the development of the School of Religious Education of which he was the first dean. From the outset he resisted the tendency to separate religious education from the mainstream of biblical, historical, theological, and pastoral education of ministers.

I learned most from Dr. Dobbins, as an organizer and construction engineer of new forms of education, as I worked with him in the development of the Department of Psychology of Religion and Pastoral Care. He and I thought of the effort to establish the clinical method of theological education as a sort of "heartbreak ridge," to use a phrase from the Korean War. I recall vividly coming with him from a particularly discouraging effort to get the director of one of our Baptist agencies in the city to see how the seminary and his institution could co-operate in the training of theological students. We had failed. The whole venture was for some reasons—probably financial and public relations—threatening to the director. We maintained his friendship, but we failed in our efforts to find a place our students could learn clinically. I was downcast as we drove up to his parking place on the campus. As I turned off the engine, I asked him, "Will we ever get this thing off the ground?"

He replied, "Yes, but we have to crawl before we can walk." Then he paused for a while, a twinkle came into his eye, and a smile came upon his face as he added, "But it does leave a particularly vulnerable part of your anatomy exposed when you are crawling, doesn't it."

Thus with humor and determination, he taught me to take defeats as being only for the day. There would be another day, another inning, another time at bat. We have lived to see the time when in the institution just mentioned and many others, we were not merely allowed to teach our students, but asked, invited, and besought.

Upon retirement, this same spirit of pioneering organization of new forms of education for students continued to fire Dr. Dobbins' imagination. He did not have time to sit and watch younger men make mistakes when he was no longer in a position to accept full responsibility alongside them. He went to Golden Gate as distinguished professor and has participated fully in the development of a brand-new school. The most recent letter I received from him was concerning the development of the new graduate program at that school. He was probing me for a bibliography of the "most recent data on graduate instruction of theological students!" I knew that he probably already had his own bibliography and just wanted to compare notes with mine.

Since Dr. Dobbins has been at Golden Gate, he has projected his capacity as an organizer on an international scale. He has served for ten years as chairman of the Commission on Bible Study and Membership Training of the Baptist World Alliance. He did not even have a mailing list of key persons responsible for Christian education in the churches when he accepted the responsibility for the Commission. Throughout most of the Baptist world, the Sunday school was looked on as an affair for children and there was nothing even resembling our Training Union. In the course of the ten years, the Baptist World Alliance has witnessed a remarkable breakthrough. At Miami Beach in 1965, when the Congress meets, the work of this Commission will play a major part. The next five years' program gives promise of almost radical change in the churches throughout much of the Baptist world.

In connection with the work of the Commission, both Dr. and Mrs. Dobbins have responded to invitations to visit Baptist bodies almost all over the world. He has held innumerable conferences, written many articles, taught intensive "brief" courses in a large number of seminaries, and carried on a huge volume of correspondence. When the books are made up, this leadership of the BWA Commission may well be looked on as his most far-reaching contribution. Since the thesis of this book is that "teachers make a difference," it is proper that reference should be made to this significant service. These are achievements of the Commission, but responsibility has rested chiefly on Dr. Dobbins.

Teaching Through Interdisciplinary Teamwork with Other Teachers

Dr. Dobbins shared his students with other teachers. He enriched his students by introducing them to other teachers. This major dimension of his teaching made a difference in my life. Within the seminary he never broke his relationship with a student who chose to work with another professor. He insisted that a graduate student fully consult with other members of the committee of instruction as well as himself. He involved his colleagues in his own teaching as much as the system at the time would permit.

Furthermore, Dr. Dobbins frequently brought other teachers into his classroom. If students had criticisms of the denominational organizations, he brought leaders of these organizations to the class to deal with these questions. I recall well having said in class that rural pastors were not involved in the writing of Sunday school and Training Union literature. It was not long before Dr. J. E. Lambdin, director of the southwide Training Union emphasis, was a visiting lecturer in our classes. I brought this issue to his attention. He asked for names of rural pastors with the proper educational credentials to write for the Training Union. The class suggested names. Later these names appeared as writers of Training Union materials.

In unexplored areas, Dr. Dobbins went outside of the Seminary for consultants. He introduced me to Chaplain Ralph Bonacker of the Norton Memorial Infirmary who gave me a full year of clinical pastoral education in co-operation with Dr. Dobbins' instructional program for me. Later, as a graduate student, Dr. Dobbins arranged an appointment and went with me to meet his long-time friend, Dr. Spafford Ackerly, Head of the Department of Psychiatry at the University of Louisville Medical School. This began a lifelong friendship and one through which I have learned more about both religion and psychiatry than I can recount here. Dr. Dobbins introduced me also to Dr. Anton T. Boisen, founder of the clinical training movement in the United States. He arranged for me to study for a summer with Dr. Boisen at Elgin State Hospital near Chicago. I did not have the money to make this venture, but Dr. Dobbins signed my note for two hundred dollars at his own bank in order that I might have this opportunity.

During these years, the most prolific writer in the field of pastoral care was Russell Dicks. Dr. Dobbins invited Russell Dicks to the campus, and we as students received the benefit of his experience as a counselor and as a writer. Russell Dicks is the man who introduced me to Paul Meacham, book editor of Westminster Press, who read the manuscript for my first book *The Christian Pastor* and decided to publish it.

I am also indebted to Dr. Dobbins for introducing me to Dr. Lewis J. Sherrill, the professor of psychology of religion and religious education at Presbyterian Theological Seminary. I later was invited by Dr. Sherrill to teach a course with him at Presbyterian Seminary at a time when I really could have profited more by taking a course from him. I learned more from Dr. Sherrill than I taught the students. Later Dr. Sherrill went to Union Theological Seminary in New York. It was he, then, who introduced me to that faculty and established a relationship with them in my behalf which has continued for fifteen years.

In short, Dr. Dobbins as a teacher brought learning and growth to greater heights by involving the student with other teachers as well as himself. In doing so, he reduced the tendency of the student to idolize him and quickened the capacity of the student to function as a junior colleague with a senior colleague in a fellowship of learning. He broadened the student's horizons beyond the province of his own relationship and increased the resources upon which the student could draw. He let no artificial lines of geography, denomination, or profession keep his student from the best leadership available in studying the problems he was trying to solve. This capacity to honor other teachers and to involve them in his students' lives as friends makes Dr. Dobbins unique among teachers. By means of this gift, he transformed my life through the new people he brought into it. This was no "technique" or "gimmick" with him. It was as much a part of him as breathing itself, for he seemed as one who had received a gift in the knowledge of these other teachers and wanted eagerly to share this gift with his students.

In a word, Dr. Dobbins was given to hospitality, but his main strength in this was Mrs. Dobbins herself. She opened her home to Dr. Dobbins' students and their families. Their living room was the scene of innumerable seminar meetings and conferences; and their table was filled with good food for students. Mrs. Dobbins knew each one of us and ministered to us as the Christian shepherdess she is. Dr. Dobbins and she set a pattern of devotion to each other which Mrs. Oates and I have sought consciously to emulate. She in a real way has been our teacher, too. In Dr. Dobbins' work she has been his protector and in his travels over the world, his companion. As he puts it, "She's a good trooper!"

Teaching Through the Discipline of Writing

Dr. Dobbins learned to work in a printing office of a newspaper. The discipline of the journalist never left him. As one who later was to write *Evangelism According to Christ*, he has remained a reporter announcing news, real news to the world. As a teacher, he hit the classroom like a headline, read a student's thesis like a hard-boiled city editor in love only with the facts, and would comment on the student's work in and out of class like a good commentator or editorial page man would. He took seriously what I wrote. He encouraged me to write. He read my thesis line for line and checked my sources. He carefully distinguished between solid writing and writing for a flowered or oratorical effect.

The real testimony to Dr. Dobbins' effectiveness as a teacher is seen in the large number of his students who have become authors in their own right, editors of Baptist papers, editors of denominational literature, and supervisors of graduate research.

I learned much from Dr. Dobbins as a writer. I learned that deadlines are to be respected with the same awe that a preacher respects eleven o'clock on Sunday morning— prepared or not, the presses have to roll! I learned that one cannot expect to get great blocks of uninterrupted time in which to write. He must learn to write amid interruptions, noise, distractions, and the demands of a heavy teaching schedule. I have interrupted Dr. Dobbins as he was typing or dictating—usually dictating—and upon finishing his conversation with me he would be dictating again before I could get the door closed on my way out. I learned also that there are many ways of getting one's material on paper. Some material must be written in longhand, other material must be typed, still other material must be dictated on a dictaphone. Dr. Dobbins uses every available means of writing. His favorite one is dictation.

Dr. Dobbins encouraged me to write with my students in mind. We needed textbook material. A professor writes as a teacher, not in order to "publish or perish." I never heard Dr. Dobbins discuss writing in terms of promotion or "getting ahead" in the academic market place. One writes in order to report what has happened, in order to provide students with written materials rather than dictating these by rote lecturing to the students to be regurgitated on tests. Students can read. They should be given materials by their teacher in written form so that they can know for certain what he thinks without the confused blurring of the note-taking process. The professor writes in order that students may have his material. He neither writes in order to be promoted nor to explain to his colleagues why he was promoted.

Dr. Dobbins often told me that another reason for writing was that a professor can multiply his student audience through the use of his materials by other teachers. Then he no longer has to depend upon the additive process of teaching the same materials to one class after another. He said, furthermore, that the publication of one's materials also involves a teacher with the thought of other teachers who respond to what he has written. Thus he becomes informed about the thought of other professors in a more personal and less wooden and "schoolboyish" way. Yet the writing ministry of Dr. Dobbins extended his influence beyond the classroom like magic. His name has become a household word among Baptist church people and his writings are now in several languages. *Building Better Churches,* for example, is now translated into Chinese.

Consequently, Dr. Dobbins as a writer wrote and still writes as a teacher and as a part of the teaching process. His writing of this present volume demonstrates the integrity of his writing ministry with his identity as a teacher. To him, writing and teaching are one, not two things. They are not functions that militate against but contribute to each other; nor can they rightly be separated from each other.

To Dr. Dobbins, it would be as incongruous to be a teacher and not to write as to be a newspaperman and not to write. He taught in the days before sabbatical leaves and did not wait until he got one to write. Nor does he live in the fond illusion that one day he will have a lodge in the Maine woods where he can retreat in order to write. The other pages of this manuscript written by Dr. Dobbins read like an exciting journalist's report of the great happenings of teachers that made a difference to him. He in turn made a difference to me as a teacher, because he took the ministry of writing and the ministry of teaching as one task. When I as a student was struggling over a manuscript, I knew that he too was struggling.

Teaching as the Presence of a Christian Gentleman

Dr. Dobbins began teaching and continued his career at Southern Seminary when teachers were not known for their kindness to students. They were known for sternness, authoritarian stance, and their capacity to put the student on the spot and make him squirm. Most of this was taken in great fun by students of the era who enjoy recounting the occasions when students were dismantled by the professors. Against the backdrop of a good measure of rough-handedness education, Dr. Dobbins' gentlemanliness and his awareness of interpersonal relationships stood in contrast.

Gaines Dobbins demonstrates all dimensions of real gentlemanliness. This includes great strength and unfailing tenderness. He makes decisions without equivocation. He stands by his decisions. He accepts leadership without hesitation. He joins battles when the issues are drawn. He holds his own in the roughest tumble a group of peers could serve up. I have seen him lay his own job on the line for principles he held dear and never flinch in the face of withering opposition and ridicule. He has unlimited qualities of loyalty to the men who serve on his staff with him. They never lack for manly protection from injustice, because he is always ready to give it.

With all of this strength, however, I have also seen Dr.

Dobbins show great gentleness. He is not given to little-ness and scrimpiness of spirit. He magnanimously prefers the good of others before his own. I think the thing that has engrained itself most profoundly in me from Dr. Dobbins' teaching has been his capacity to stand frustration without losing composure. By nature, temperament, and cultural background, I have never been a person who could tolerate incompetence, injustice, or unreasonable frustration without considerable loss of patience, composure, and temper. As a result, I can honestly say that the example of Christian forbearance, patience, and tolerance which Dr. Dobbins conveyed to me more than once made the difference in my acting hastily and ill-advisedly and my acting discreetly, soberly, and in the fear of God. I found in Dr. Dobbins an example of trust, permissiveness with my impatience, and a remarkable gentling effect. With all his shrewdness and courage in dealing forthrightly with people, I never detected a shred of ruthlessness in him. From him I learned the measure of a Christian gentleman who lives intimately with God. From him I learned that there is such a thing as the residue of original sin in both seminary students and professors and that there is no substitute either for the wisdom of the serpents nor for the harmlessness of the doves as one decided to give his life to theological education. As my intellectual parent in Christ, then, Dr. Dobbins is a teacher who made a difference in my life. He has been a father to me but has never treated me as a child. The reason is that he sees himself as a child of God in Christ.

As I wrote him upon his departure to Golden Gate on March 5, 1956, I tried to put these feelings into words:

You have been my parent in the faith and work of our Lord Jesus Christ. You will always be, no matter where you are. You have believed in me when I had no longer any belief in myself. You have both found me for the task that is mine and helped me to find myself in it. Apart from your dedication and courage, my efforts would have been in vain in the field you have bequeathed to me. The fact that I did not lose my way I owe to your experience, pioneering insight, matchless skill and intrepid faith. I shall be a good soldier in the stewardship of that which I have inherited from you.

The fact that you are going to Golden Gate is consistent with the structure of God's image in you. You will always be a pioneer and for that reason you will have that abounding flow of fresh meaning that keeps life sweet and vital. You have been to me the sterling example of a Christian gentleman, a thing so much a part of you that I have never seen you do an ignoble, uncharitable, or ungentlemanly thing. You have always in honor preferred the other, done the magnanimous thing. When God poured the greatness of his heart on Southern Baptists, he tilted the pan a bit in your direction. For in taking the lowest place and the hardest place, the fulness of God has overflowed upon you!

9
You Too Can Be
a Great Teacher

In the course of nearly half a century of teaching I have had approximately ten thousand students pass through my seminary classes. My Ridgecrest and Glorieta alumni would total an almost countless multitude. In all seriousness I have tried to convey to them this message: *You too can be a great teacher*.

"Oh, no," most of them have smiled back at me as if to say, "we have no such illusion." In the context of these profiles of great teachers, they may in effect have said: "We never expect to attain the insightfulness of a Mullins, the versatility of a Sampey, the erudition of a Robertson, the originality of a Carver, the social conscience of a Gardner, the editorial skill of a Van Ness, or the person-mindedness of a Coe."

The Great Teachers' Test

They made a difference! The disclaimer may well be conceded. These men possessed an excellence that set them apart. But the principle by which their greatness may be measured is applicable to the humblest teachers: *they made a difference*. The extent or degree of that difference may be greater than that of the notable teacher if measured in terms of notice and acclaim, but in God's hall of fame the obscure teacher may rate ahead of the most famous teacher by man's standards.

It is not always easy to determine whether the teacher and his teaching are making a difference. In the factors that bring change to human life are many indeterminates. Who shifted life-direction toward and to Christ? In the course of events, who turned the trend upward? At a time of crisis, who weighted the scales that resulted in a destiny-determining decision? A complex of influences may have been at work. Yet when the incidental is sifted from the fundamental, the chances are that a teacher made the difference. The teacher may never have been in a classroom situation and the teaching may not have been derived from books, but the relation was that of teacher-learner, and because of this relationship life became different. Not until the books are balanced in the final judgment may the facts be known. Teachers may rest assured that their part will be significant and will be recognized.

The teacher's greatness may not be measured by the number of persons taught. Houston Peterson edited a book titled *Great Teachers*. He chose twenty contemporary teachers who deserved to be in the list; then he requested a notable student of each of these teachers to write the appreciative biographical sketch.

At the head of the list is the name of Anne Mansfield Sullivan. Her sole student was Helen Keller. Miss Sullivan was herself a handicapped child. Born of poverty-stricken immigrant Irish parents, her father a drunkard, her mother an undernourished invalid, and she herself almost blind with trachoma, Anne Sullivan at the age of ten became a ward of the state of Massachusetts. As such she came to the attention of Dr. Samuel Gridley Howe, director of the Perkins Institution for the Blind. Here she learned the manual alphabet, recovered partial use of her eyesight, and was graduated at the age of twenty as valedictorian of her class.

Then came the appeal to become the teacher of a blind, deaf, and mute child in Alabama. Responding eagerly, she undertook the almost impossible task of breaking through the stony silence and the midnight darkness of this child who could neither hear nor see nor speak. Anne Sullivan's greatness as teacher rests on the difference she made in the life of this blind-deaf-mute child, her only pupil for a lifetime.

Houston Peterson writes in the introduction:

The more I think about it, the better this [story of Anne Mansfield Sullivan] seems as the opening essay. Does it seem too far-fetched to picture the young Helen Keller as the symbol par excellence of every student that ever lived? We are all Helen Kellers in some degree—vision beclouded, ears undiscriminating, speech uncertain and untrue. We have all needed, at one time or another, to have *truth* spelled out slowly for us, to have our capabilities redefined and re-evaluated, and the limitations of our sensations and perceptions suggested. It is no mean epitaph for any teacher to have it said of him that "he rendered all whom he taught less deaf, less dumb, less blind." [1]

Your Test: Do You Make a Difference?

The greatness of the teacher does not stem so much from what he himself accomplished as from the attain-

---

[1] *Great Teachers* (New Brunswick, N. J.: Rutgers University Press, 1946), pp. 20–21.

ments of his students. Socrates was Plato's teacher, awakening the powers of one of the greatest of the ancient philosophers; Plato was Aristotle's teacher, stimulating the intellectual development of the philosopher who shaped the course of intellectual history for more than two milleniums; Aristotle was the teacher of Alexander the Great, who changed the direction of political history from the fourth century B.C. to the modern age. Contemporary examples without number could be cited to prove the point—the teacher is known by the students he influences. Men and women in high places in all walks of life bear grateful testimony to obscure teachers.

A teacher's greatness is not measured necessarily by his scholarship. Originally, a scholar was simply a learner, a pupil; presently the word applies to the man of exceptional learning. To be sure, the teacher must possess a fund of knowledge, but he may have very limited erudition and yet possess elements of true greatness. On the other hand, the teacher with vast learning may be a relative failure.

What the teacher knows is more important than what he knows about. A teacher who knows God but has a very elementary knowledge of theology may rate as a better teacher than one who is a master of theology but does not know God through an experience of repentance and faith. Every teacher is under obligation to gain as much mastery as possible of his subject; but if the subject is the Christian religion, the teacher's highest qualification is not to be master of subject matter but to be mastered by the Christ whose subject he is. This explains why teachers with meager formal education, doing their best with what they have, may nevertheless be rated as great teachers.

Skill in the techniques of teaching is not a necessary qualification of the great teacher. This is not to depreciate the importance of good method. However effective the teacher may be without the knowledge and use of sound method, he would be more successful if his teaching reflected tested methodology. Method, however, is not a substitute for dynamic faith in God or sincere love of people. Given these two qualities, the teacher who teaches "by ear," knowing little of formal pedagogy, may earn the title to greatness which the skilled technician, lacking these qualities, may miss.

The price of becoming a great teacher includes dedication, sweat of brain, concentration, sacrifice, determination, the practice of prayer, imagination, love of people, consecration. These abstractions take on definite meaning when in a definite situation practice is according to sound theory. As great teachers are studied and emulated, the question persists: *Why and how did they make a difference?*

Within your own sphere, with your limitations and abilities, with the resources available, according to the will of God in Christ, under the guidance of the Holy Spirit, you too can be a great teacher!

Share Your Appreciations

To appreciate is to value—to be conscious of significance. Everyone has a scale of values, a measure of significance. Perhaps nothing reveals a man's character more than what he appreciates. Scarcely anything that a teacher may do is more important than to share his appreciations with his students. In the sharing, if the teacher enhances both his and their sense of values, he will have rendered an inestimable service.

One of the most delightful of William Lyon Phelps's essays is on *Appreciation.* "The curse of modern life," he writes, "the poison that turns honey to gall, because of the dull, stupid, dependent mood in which so many people live and move and have their being, is a lack of appreciation. Many go through life with their eyes, ears, and minds closed." [2]

In a personal conversation with Dr. Phelps, when he was approaching his eightieth birthday, I asked the secret of his freshness and vitality.

"If I have a secret," he replied, "it is this: I have never met a person who was not interesting."

Is not this the mark of the great teacher and the high level of appreciation—to see worth in every person and to value every person for his own sake?

The near-fatal mistake of a teacher is to teach *lessons* rather than *persons.* When this occurs, the student assumes to the teacher the "I-it" relationship instead of the "I-thou." This quality of respect for personality characterized Jesus Christ supremely. His person-mindedness shines out in every individual encounter. He was as concerned for the disreputable Samaritan woman as he was for the renowned Nicodemus. Even when he dealt severely with the Pharisees, it was because he sought their welfare. More than any other teacher, Jesus taught the infinite worth of personality, regardless of race, class, or condition.

Because the teacher has the mind of Christ concerning

---

[2] William Lyon Phelps, *Appreciation* (New York: E. P. Dutton & Co., 1932), pp. 16–17.

persons, he values truth, goodness, and beauty. As he shares these appreciations in the context of his relationship to Christ, he consciously and unconsciously enhances the appreciations of his students. In so doing, he puts himself within the circle of the great teachers, no matter how inconspicuous he may feel his place of service to be.

Share Your Insights

Admittedly the Bible is a difficult book to teach and to learn. Its language of a distant past must be translated, its framework of history must be recovered, its patterns of thought must be interpreted, its references and allusions must be researched. Painstaking effort is required to gather the facts, to search for meanings, to determine the setting, and to translate Hebrew and Greek concepts into modern thought patterns. In the midst of this sort of study with a view to teaching, the teacher may bog down. The materials to be taught may seem cold, uninteresting, irrelevant, unteachable. The class may be even more befogged.

At this point of frustration there is need of *insight*. Not only is this the gift of the "inspired" thinker, it is a way open to all who aspire to be creative teachers.

Eliot Dole Hutchinson describes the tedious process of research into a problem that reaches a dead end:

But suddenly, usually in a moment when the work has been temporarily abandoned or when the attention is absorbed by irrelevant matters, comes an unpredicted *insight* into the solution. As if "inspired," "given," apparently effortless, arise ideas which constitute a real integration of previously accumulated experience—an answer, a brilliant hypothesis, a useful "hunch," forming, it seems, a short cut to artistic or scientific advance. Exhilaration marks such moments of insight; a glow or elation goes with them. They are characterized by a feeling of adequacy, finality, accomplishment.[3]

Dr. Mullins once told me how he came to write *Axioms of Religion.* He was struggling with the problem of a fresh, convincing approach to the Baptist position. His accumulated notes from wide reading had left him frustrated, cold. One night as he sat reading, suddenly there came to him the idea of stating the Baptist position in terms of axioms, self-evident truths, and by midnight he had devised the framework of the book.

Teaching, especially Bible teaching, requires more than sight—it demands *insight.* After having read what others say, after having studied text and context, the teacher may turn to prayerful meditation, asking for divine guidance in the discovery of meanings that have been hidden from view. The answer may not come at once and frustration may deepen. But patient faith will have its reward and light will break. Sharing this illumination with his students, the teacher will make a contribution richer and more meaningful than narration of events or the reciting of facts. The insightful teacher will stimulate to insightfulness on the part of the class and this process of sharing of insights is the mark of the great teacher.

Share Your Enthusiasm

The teacher with sustained enthusiasm has a priceless possession. Teaching may be thought of as a game in which the teacher is trying to win out over ignorance, error, in-

---

[3] *How to Think Creatively* (Nashville: Abingdon–Cokesbury Press, 1949), p. 18.

difference, pride, prejudice. In the competition, an ounce of enthusiasm may be worth a pound of cold sense.

Enthusiasm is not to be confused with noisy gusto, ecstatic speech, frenzied zeal, high-pitched ardor, extravagant fervor—predominance of the emotional over the intellectual. By *enthusiasm*, the Greeks meant the indwelling of divinity, possession by a god, hence inspired and upheld by a spiritual influence. Christ expressed it when he said, "He who abides in me, and I in him, he it is that bears much fruit, for apart from me you can do nothing" (John 15:5, RSV).

Paul's concept was that of "Christ in you, the hope of glory" (Col. 1:27). Paul's enthusiasm for Christ sustained him in his hardships and sufferings, in his defeats and disappointments, in the dark hours of his imprisonment, as well as in his joys and victories.

Dr. Sampey often spoke of the teacher's "drive." He was not thinking of the teacher as a slave driver but as forging ahead, undiscouraged, toward his objective. He himself embodied this quality in high degree. It is within the possibility of every teacher to acquire and develop this divine attribute of enthusiasm. To do so is to join the ranks of the great teachers.

Share Your Learning

Ignorance may be excused on the part of members of the class, but preventable ignorance is inexcusable on the part of the teacher. James warns that not everyone should undertake to be a teacher, "for you know that we who teach shall be judged with greater strictness" (James 3:1, RSV). The call to be a teacher is the call to thorough preparation. One need not be an outstanding scholar in order to teach. But no one has a right to be called teacher who is not willing to take seriously his responsibility for learning all he can.

Dr. Robertson was upset when he discovered students, who were going out to be teachers, unwilling to pay the price of learning. On an occasion he cried out in distress, "How can I inspire these men to learn? How can they expect to preach the Book unless they know it?" He knew that mastery of the New Testament came through concentrated study—there is no other way.

To share is to partake or enjoy with others. It is not sharing if there is no mutual give-and-take. The teacher is not sharing who transmits what *he* has learned to a nonparticipating class. The teacher who has discovered the joy of learning must communicate his discovery to his students.

The teacher learns; he stimulates his students to learn; what both have learned they share in the teaching-learning process. The formula runs thus: much sharing, much learning; little sharing, little learning; no sharing, no learning.

The teacher would not have been appointed to his post had he not been capable of learning. He must assume that every person in the class is likewise capable of learning. The more he stimulates learning activity, the more fully he enters into the ranks of the great teachers.

Share Your Concern for Human Welfare

The teacher is under inescapable obligation to put his teaching into practice. How can one presume to teach the Bible and ignore its practical application to human beings? When Peter, witnessing to Cornelius, the Roman soldier, spoke to him of Jesus Christ, he described him as anointed with the Holy Spirit and with power. The evidence was that he "went about doing good and healing all that were oppressed by the devil" (Acts 10:38, RSV). "Doing good" is not the price of salvation but it is its evidence.

There are monstrous forces of evil that continue to oppress the people. There are diseases that cripple both body and mind that need healing. There are social injustices that cry to heaven for correction. "Teaching the Bible" is more than exposure to its truths—teaching is incomplete until the truths taught have carried over into social action.

The teacher who has the mind of Christ will have a sensitive social conscience. He will not only be on the side of justice, he will throw himself into the struggle that righteousness may win. This does not necessarily mean crusading for a particular cause, but it does mean sending students out into the world so taught that in social and economic and political issues they will stand up and be counted. The teacher who makes no application of the Bible to issues involving human welfare may be compared to the beatnik "rebel without a cause."

Such men as Charles S. Gardner and George Albert Coe clearly saw that the Bible must be taught in the present tense, as Christianity today, not Christianity yesterday. They realized and caused their students to realize that the gospel must make a difference not only in persons but also in their environment. In this they followed in the footsteps of the great teachers of the ages, supremely Jesus Christ, the greatest of teachers. The teacher who thus awakens Christian conscience and directs it into channels of betterment for men everywhere belongs in the circle of the great.

Share Your Concern for the Kingdom

The Christian teacher belongs to a church; his church is affiliated with a denomination; the denomination is related to other Christian bodies; but overarching all is the kingdom of God. The initial proclamation of Jesus was not concerning the church or the denomination but the kingdom. He "came . . . preaching the gospel of God, and saying, 'The time is fulfilled, and the kingdom of God is at hand; repent, and believe in the gospel'" (Mark 1:14–15, RSV). He almost exhausted language and figures of speech to tell of the kingdom—its meaning, its worth, its nature, its supremacy.

To become a Christian is to enter this kingdom. To serve and grow as a Christian is to expand one's relation to the kingdom, to bring the kingdom to others, and to bring others into the kingdom. Concern for the kingdom of God marks the beginning of the Christian life and is its ultimate end, for no spiritual concept can go beyond "the reign of God in Christ in the lives of all men everywhere."

When Jesus taught his disciples to pray, "Thy kingdom come . . . on earth as it is in heaven," he defined the Christian's responsibility as including all of humanity in all areas of life. The teacher will, therefore, be mission-minded and will miss no opportunity to relate his teaching to the missionary enterprise. "On earth as . . . in heaven" begins with concern to reach the unreached in the community, beyond to the unevangelized of the state, still further to the unsaved of the nation, and across the seas to those who sit in darkness and the shadow of death even "unto the uttermost part." No teacher of the Bible can be a truly great teacher who does not have this "from—to" perspective. Whoever has this evangelistic-missionary devotion is a great teacher, whatever may be his limitations.

Concern for the kingdom marks the teacher in a closer circle of responsibility and opportunity. Jesus compared the kingdom to seed sown in soil. Some seeds failed the crucial test—they did not reproduce themselves. Other seeds met the test—they reproduced abundantly.

The teacher of children, looking back over the years, may well ask: How many of these children have grown up to be teachers, ministers, missionaries, leaders of Christian thought and action?

Teachers of young people and adults may test their teaching with the question: How many class members have responded to the call of the church to become teachers, officers, leaders in the life of the church, of the denomination, of the community, of state and nation? The teacher who can count a significant number of those who have been influenced by his shared concern for the kingdom to occupy places of usefulness and responsibility in the church and beyond, however humble or notable the place, belongs in the ranks of the great.

Central in concern for the kingdom is concern for individual persons. "There is joy before the angels of God over one sinner who repents" (Luke 15:10, RSV). The good shepherd left the ninety-nine sheep that were safe in the fold and sought the one sheep that was lost. Bringing lost men into the kingdom is not a wholesale transaction but a concentration on winning one person at a time.

Here is the teacher's crown of greatness: to have Jesus Christ himself join the class and, through the "miracle of

dialogue," use the biblical revelation to transform un-
believers and to send out believers to share this experience
with others. No Christian teacher can be counted great
who falls short of this objective. Any teacher is a great
teacher who, by sharing his experience of salvation, brings
others to the Saviour.

When Dr. Luther Wesley Smith retired from his position
as executive secretary of the American Baptist Publication
Society, he had made an investment of a near lifetime of
service to Bible school teachers. He had dreamed dreams
that had become realities. Luella Killion Funk paid tribute
to this teacher of teachers in words that may well apply
to any teacher who has shared himself and his dreams
with others in the noble company of those who have
followed in the train of the Great Teacher:

> One need not sleep to dream!
> And they who walk today
> Where dreams have been fulfilled,
> Or, in the process of fulfillment,
> Are witness to that power divine
> Which plays upon the souls of men
> Who seek to do His will,
> To follow in His way.
>
> Across the trails of cool doubt
> With work and prayer and tears,
> They build in faith;
> And in the building wait that hour
> When to the real the vision thus
>   translated
> Becomes a Holy thing indeed.
> One cannot sleep and dream! [4]

[4] *Baptist Leader*, April, 1964.